Mel — with affectionate
regards from Geo.

Man and Metaphysics

WOODBRIDGE LECTURES

NUMBER TWO

DELIVERED AT COLUMBIA UNIVERSITY

1947

Man and Metaphysics

GEORGE P. ADAMS *1882*

MILLS PROFESSOR OF MENTAL AND
MORAL PHILOSOPHY AND CIVIL POLITY
UNIVERSITY OF CALIFORNIA

COLUMBIA UNIVERSITY PRESS
New York, 1948

48·7412

Preface

THIS SMALL VOLUME COMPRISES THE Woodbridge Lectures delivered at Columbia University in the spring of 1947. The original lecture form has been retained and the lectures are here printed substantially as they were given.

Man's concern with an understanding of his own life and nature and of the total context in which his life is lived has come to possess for us an almost unprecedented urgency and pathos. With respect to this perennially central undertaking of philosophical reflection, the point of view which finds utterance in these lectures is probably at variance with the dominant climate of opinion in recent and contemporary philosophy. The "revolt against dualism" and the opposition to any "bifurcation" of man and nature or mind and nature is still gathering momentum.

Yet I should not wish that the views here set forth should be summarily subsumed under any traditional rubric of "dualism" or of "idealism." Nevertheless, the persuasion that there is that in man and in the human spirit which holds intimations of a dimension of being other than that of nature is the central theme of these chapters. Man's sense of the claims made upon his life and thought by that which transcends the phenomenal and empirical order of nature's events, I call his metaphysical sense.

Man hath what Nature hath and more,
And in that more lie all his hopes of good.

It is this "more" that I am concerned with in this book.

I do not think it incongruous that the book in which this concern finds expression should be dedicated to the memory of Professor Woodbridge. It was never my privilege to have had him as a teacher. Nearly thirty years ago the University of California borrowed him for a semester from Columbia, and it was there that I came to know him. We gave him a plain little office, quite unlike the one with which I was so generously provided at Columbia. We had something of the feeling when he came that he was a little homesick and that nothing which we could offer him by way of fog and sunshine quite compensated for the things that he missed. We discovered very early that he liked to have us come and talk with him. This we did, and it was not we who needed to do very much of the talking; for a chance comment or question would release a fund of learning and insight, imagination and wisdom, uttered with trenchant pungency as his restless mind played freely with the wealth of ideas with which he lived and which he had made his own. All of this, and more, those who lived with him for years know better than do I.

And I discover in his writings, as I read and reread them, a metaphysical imagination responsive to a profound sense of that "more" which belongs to man, together with a scrupulous concern that nature be deprived of nothing which is her due. What comments he himself might have made to the things I am about to say, I do not know or, perhaps I should say, I do know. I can still see the quizzical but kindly gleam in his eyes.

GEORGE P. ADAMS

September 12, 1947

Contents

Man and Metaphysics

CHAPTER I

Life and Knowledge

THE HISTORY OF MAN'S PURSUIT OF PHI-
losophy warns us not to delimit with too fine a precision the territory which philosophy may claim for
its own. There is no major aspect or province of man's
world, or of his own career and life, which has not provided
grist for some philosopher's mill. It is unwise to legislate
in advance as to what may properly fall to the lot of the
scientist, the historian, the theologian, or the philosopher.
Nor, to judge from its history, can any unambiguous statement be made as to the impact which philosophy is intended to have upon man's life, or as to the absence of any
such impact.

Is philosophy primarily critical, ready and eager to show
how fragile are the grounds upon which men base their
beliefs and their loyalties, how tenuous and flimsy are the
ideas which have become woven into the fabric of the
common sense of mankind, into their morals and religion,
their institutions, and all the substantive ingredients of
man's way of living—ideas in terms of which he may think
to organize his life? Or is philosophy a speculative and constructive enterprise, yielding some final and global conspectus, providing unassailable premises and solid foundations,
without which life would be rudderless and chartless?

Is it, for instance, the province of the philosopher to tell
the scientist that he, the scientist, has no warrant for carry-

ing on his activities, as scientist, until the philosopher has provided him with his basic premises and presuppositions from which the sciences take off and upon which they must build? And if the sciences are not beholden to philosophy for the charter which guarantees their rights and privileges, which authorizes and justifies their procedures, must we not grant a similar autonomy to morals and religion, to art and politics, and to the thousand activities which make up the stuff and substance of human living? What business has philosophy to intrude into the energies and activities displayed in man's life and experience?

Ever since Socrates talked with Protagoras, Gorgias, and Theaetetus, with playful irony and sustained earnestness, the belief that philosophy has a mission to perform, pertinent and germane to every facet within the entire venture of man's life, has never been absent. There was no doubt in the mind of Socrates or his successors as to what was the essential nature of this mission. It was to illumine all of life with knowledge and insight, even if it be only the knowledge that life is not in possession of the insight which it ought to have if it is to meet the requirements of our human way of living. Socrates would wish that men, engaged in the activities of the market place, the public square, the shop and laboratory, should pause and ask of themselves the question, What can I know concerning what I am doing, its meaning, the direction that life is taking, the ends which it is pursuing, and the validity of the principles that life exhibits and employs? Thus to pause, to cease, as it were, to engage in the concrete activities of living, to reflect, is a kind of withdrawal from life. But such withdrawal and detachment are required if one is to know, and not just to live. The exigencies and urgencies which subtend the activities in which life engages, the anxieties, cares, and practical con-

cerns of life—all of the immediacies of action are incon-
sistent with the poise and detachment needful for knowing.

A conception of the meaning and nature of the activity of
knowing, at least of its intent, which sets this activity apart
from all of the practical and vital activities in which men engage, begins to take shape. Knowing is the activity of a
spectator who has drawn himself away from the necessities
of action. He stands at a distance from the scene which he
would know and encompass by means of his vision. The
framework and perspective within which men live and act
and interact with all the multiform things and processes
within which their living is caught up, this perspective
becomes subject to a drastic dislocation when the intent to
seek knowledge comes upon the scene of human life. A
sense of the contrast and discrepancy between knowing and
doing, between theory and practice, between a spectator
and an active participant, between knowledge and life, becomes articulate in the philosophy of Plato and Aristotle.
Through them it is injected into the stream and tradition
of European philosophy, either to nourish and to sustain it
or perchance to divert it into channels leading to waywardness, confusion, and aridity.

The paradox inherent in the conviction common to
Socrates, Plato, and Aristotle lies just here. Philosophy can
perform its proper service for life only by withdrawing from
life, by sustaining the attitude and activity of an onlooker, a
spectator. For this is what it means to seek knowledge and
to know. But life itself requires knowledge if it is to be the
kind of life suitable to man. Human living is in need of that
which cannot be supplied from within the resources belonging to the activities of life itself, of life as the congeries of
vital and practical interests. The metaphysics of Plato and
Aristotle issues from the attempt to think through the im-

plications of this paradox. What is there in man that can sufficiently detach itself from the demands made by life so as to become a spectator and to acquire the knowledge which life requires? What kind of a world is it which can elicit and sustain this intent to know and the activity of knowing, of scanning the contours of life and of existence as a spectator? What is it that man may know as a spectator which bears upon his living and which will enable him to organize his life and his society in ways that are consonant with the good which he may discern? Ethics and politics become caught up within the framework of the metaphysics which proffers answers to questions such as these.

There is, then, ample justification for such a statement as that made by J. L. Stocks, that "in almost every sense that can legitimately be given to an overworked and much abused word, the ancient Greeks are entitled to the description 'rationalist.' With them the dominant tendency from the beginning to the end of their creative period was the assertion of the power of thought to find unassailable truth and to organize individual and social life in accordance with the findings." [1]

Within the framework of a philosophy such as this, all life and experience becomes dependent upon knowledge and insight, so far as concerns the validity of the premises and principles upon which man's experience is based, and the ends which life pursues. Life and experience are not autonomous. They are so far dependent upon knowledge as almost to become incidents and episodes within a sustained cognitive venture. All of man's living and experience is viewed as a kind of medium and vehicle through which being is disclosed, however darkly and falteringly. All of experience is, with varying degrees of adequacy, cognitive. All

[1] *Time, Cause and Eternity* (London, 1938), p. 5.

of experience is the bearer of a message which may be clearly read, to be sure, only when the mind withdraws from action and life and becomes a spectator. What are virtue and moral excellence but a kind of knowledge, and moral perversity but a kind of blindness and ignorance? Throughout all of its ranges, man's life and experience may become the medium through which knowledge and insight are to be sought and attained. Yet the duality and tension between thought and action, theory and practice, knowledge and life are not annulled. To know is to be a spectator, to withdraw from action; to live is to engage in the specific vital and practical activities called for by the necessities of one's nature and one's circumstances.

No reminder is needed that the massive, formative forces which have shaped European life and thought since Socrates conversed with his friends have profoundly altered men's ideas about the relation between knowledge and life. The dominant forces, resident within both their experience and their knowledge have brought about, during the last four or five hundred years, a complete reversal of the premises and tenets of Greek rationalism. Instead of assigning to knowledge the role of eliciting and judging the meaning and the validity of man's life and experience, a knowledge dependent upon the activity of a spectator, it is to life and experience that we now give primacy. Knowledge ceases to be the judge of what life and experience are or should become. Knowledge is ancillary to life. Within the framework supplied by this perspective, the activity of knowing becomes a phase and episode of life and living. The meaning and worth of experience in all its reaches ceases to be dependent upon any insight derived from what a spectator might discern. Knowing becomes one specific way of living. Like breathing and digesting, its function is to minister to the fulfillment of life's needs and requirements. Knowledge is inserted into life and, since living is an affair of sustaining a vital interchange and interaction between the living organism and its habitat within a world embracing them both, the activity of knowing is now viewed as a specific and special set of occurrences within the framework of that common world. The spectator view of knowledge together with the entire edifice which it has supported ceases to be a live option. The relation between life and knowledge has become reversed.

The forms which this momentous reversal has taken on, within the world both of thought and of action, are protean. Are the bounds of plausibility overshot if it is said that many of the currents, both of knowledge and life, which may be subsumed under the rubric of romanticism, irrationalism, or mysticism, are symptoms and outcroppings of this reversal? What are thought, reason, and knowledge that they should hold life and experience in bondage? Why should these exuberant, vital energies receive their sanction from anything provided by knowledge? They are autonomous. They may use such knowledge as may prove serviceable for their demands, but they are sovereign, neither asking nor receiving from knowledge any charter to guarantee their meaning and validity, least of all any sanction derived from a spectator detached from the immediacies of life and action.

I have associated the two terms "life" and "experience." That conjunction is significant. It will point our way, somewhat later, to an understanding of what is covered and denoted by the term "experience," and to a recognition of the contrast between what belongs to experience and what does not. The term "experience" carries an accent of modernity. I know of no Greek word which is quite its equivalent. The nearest, perhaps, is ζωή, "life," particularly as it is used in the New Testament, and here we have already moved beyond the frontiers of classical Greek metaphysics. Whatever the meaning and content of "experience" may turn out to be, the autonomy and ultimacy of experience is, of course, the premise of empiricism. And we rightly take empiricism to be a name for such philosophies as have captured and given expression to the meaning and drift of tendencies distinctly modern.

Modern empiricisms, then, comprise a chapter, or a series of chapters, in the history of this reversal in the relative position of life and knowledge. Echoes of the spectator view of knowledge linger on, but the logic implicit in the premises supplied by this reversal drives it further and further into the background. The cards are stacked initially against the possibility of the kind of detachment from the immediacies of life and experience which could make possible and significant the vocation of a spectator. Knowledge springs from experience, arises within experience, is beholden to experience for its title and claim to be knowledge. Life and experience do not, as for the Greek thinkers, hold their title from knowledge and insight.

The earlier classical empiricists, Bacon, Locke, and Berkeley, are hesitant in thinking through the implications of this primacy of life and experience. Were I to name the one classical modern philosopher who most clearly saw the nature and meaning of this reversal, I should unhesitatingly choose Hume. Hume's philosophy is not skepticism. His position would have been that of skepticism had he supposed that it was the business of knowledge to validate the activities of life and experience. Knowledge cannot do this, and it should not be asked to do this. Life and experience require nothing other than themselves to insure their own integrity and significance. They rest on no foundations or premises which knowledge can or should be expected to supply or to justify. They are sovereign and autonomous, and knowledge is their servant. Reason is a slave of the passions. The cool, analytic mind of Hume, probing with consummate skill into man's nature and experience, seems miles removed from any outlook or temper suggested by such terms as romanticism or irrationalism. But Hume's belief that life and experience owe no allegiance to reason and knowledge brings his philosophy much closer to these currents of life and thought than might at first be supposed. Hume's philosophy is a declaration of independence on the part of life and experience, an implicit disavowal of the audacious claim of Socrates that all of life should be subject to the jurisdiction of that which only knowledge can supply. Hume reaches the conclusion that so far as the premises, the organizing principles, and the meaning of life and experience are concerned philosophy is expendable. The fruitful pursuit of knowledge lies elsewhere. Men may observe and, in a way, learn and know much that is curious and useful. But the currents of man's living have a momentum and a range which carry them beyond any orbit within which knowledge, let alone philosophy, may hope to move. The Humean position marks the polar antithesis of the Socratic conviction. The reversal of the relation between life and knowledge has become complete.

These broad, much too broad, generalizations which I have made supply the background for the questions with which these chapters will be concerned. There is man, his life, his career, his enactments, his experience; and there is knowledge, in any case the pursuit of knowledge. There are the sciences and there is metaphysics. What shall we make of this reversal of the relation between life and knowledge as we go from Socrates to Hume? It is sometimes thought to be a scandal that philosophy should be so much preoccupied with the problem of knowledge and of knowing, instead of seeking what it is that men may know about themselves and their world. Is knowing an activity any more mysterious than walking and breathing? It may indeed be marvelous that nature should have implanted in the body a wisdom which enables it to sustain its vital activities. Why not let knowing be greeted with the same natural piety? To detach knowing—some knowing at least—from life and action, as did the Greeks, to make of the mind a *speculum* and a spectator, appears to shut the doors against any comprehension of the role played by knowing and its organ in nature's economy. Clearly all these matters thicken into the question as to what manner of thing the mind is, and what manner of existence it enjoys. Man has pursued metaphysics. Metaphysics is a product of his thinking, reflection, and imagination. And the metaphysics which issues from these activities is to embrace the source from which it has come.

The ideas and beliefs to which the adjectives "philosophical" or "metaphysical" are attached belong to a somewhat different order from those ideas and theories which we commonly call "scientific." Philosophy lies somewhat nearer life, our common life, than does science, in spite of the fact that our own life and habits of thought have been so vastly transformed by science. For instance, beyond the rudiments of elementary arithmetic, say the multiplication table, mathematics is not a common human possession. In coming to the study of differential equations the student enters upon a world of ideas of which the common man, concerned with the business of living, has not the slightest inkling. There is indeed some thread, long and tenuous, which links the refinements and techniques of mathematical analysis with ordinary experience and common sense. And there is a road which leads back from differential equations to the harnessing of nature, to engineering and technology, a road traversed by a small number of experts. Philosophy too has its refinements, its niceties of analysis, its exploration of ideas, to be pursued and enjoyed with sheer intellectual delight by the few who may make of it a vocation or an avocation.

But, somewhat unlike mathematics and the prodigious refinements of all the other sciences, philosophical ideas and beliefs, persuasions and commitments, are about something with which man's life and experience are wholly familiar. Every man has some sense, however vague and inarticulate, of the direction and setting of his life; he has some notion, however confused, of the scheme of things in the midst of which he finds himself. Man not only lives, in the sense of meeting the exigencies of the moment as do all animals; he becomes aware of his life and of distant stretches of his world, even if but vaguely and fitfully. To have some philosophy is a human prerogative.

Had nature intended that man's acquistion of knowledge should be harnessed solely to the furtherance of ends supplied by life, but the validity of which is not subject to the scrutiny of thought and reflection, she did a curious and surprising thing in permitting him even to imagine that he might withdraw from life, scrutinize his life as a spectator, and subject all of his enterprises to criteria not entirely fetched from the vital and practical demands indigenous to the business of living. We have come to know too much about the contingent and irrational sources, the biological, historical, and social roots of our beliefs and loyalties, to commit ourselves to them with innocent and zealous con-

viction. Animals other than man have been spared such
knowledge and awareness, such "conscience" as "does make
cowards of us all."

There is another difference between metaphysical beliefs and those which have the authenticity of science. No
conspectus of man's life and of his world, such as philosophy
may think to provide, is of the same order as the belief, or
knowledge, that sugar is soluble in water, or that I ought
to have the batteries of my car recharged. For beliefs such as
these the evidence is specific and definite. The ideas about
sugar and batteries are verifiable. The evidence at hand supplies an objective basis both for prediction and for control
of our practical common sense and, when enormously refined and expanded, of the laboratory technician and the
experimental scientist. We are living in an age which is profoundly impressed by the prodigious achievements and the
unlimited possibilities of procedures based upon this appeal to and utilization of specific evidence. The prestige of
science has accorded to it an unprecedentedly privileged
position, comparable to that enjoyed by theology in an
earlier period now lying almost wholly in the past. This
prestige prompts us to ask the question whether all of the
beliefs and persuasions by which men live, so far as their
truth or validity is concerned, should not be made equally
dependent uopn such specific evidence as gives support to
the beliefs of common sense and of science.

Philosophical and metaphysical beliefs appear to be due
to factors other than the evidence upon which beliefs of the
order of science are based. Evidence is something that is
there, denotable, objective, accessible, and public. It lies in
front of the mind. Philosophical ideas and beliefs exhibit
the influence of pressures which play upon the mind from
behind. A scientific idea or belief is, we say, determined by

and is faithful to the evidence alone. Philosophical beliefs
are the resultant and expression of something antecedent to
the objective evidence. Lying behind rather than in front
of the mind, they escape notice. They operate in the dark.
The current vogue of the term "climate of opinion" serves
to call attention to one such large-scale determinant of belief not there in front of the mind as objective evidence, but
coloring and shaping our judgments none the less. All of us,
including philosophers, live and think within some specific
climate of opinion. Intellectual climates change, and we
can best characterize specific historical epochs not so much
by specific beliefs as by the climate of opinion which nour-
ishes and sustains all beliefs. Professor Becker has, for instance, depicted the striking contrast between the medieval
climate of opinion and that within which the modern mind
lives and carries on its thinking. "The modern mind, which
curiously notes and carefully describes everything, can indeed describe this [medieval] climate of opinion, although
it cannot live in it." [2] One may wonder how adequate one's
understanding of an alien climate of opinion will be when
it is thus viewed by an external observer who is unable, in
imagination, to place himself within that climate. In any
case the climate of opinion is a large-scale, pervasive determinant of men's thinking. There are other forces which
press upon the pattern of our thinking from behind. There
is the philosopher's own individual sensitivity to particular
strands and ingredients in life and experience. He is impressed by the range and significance of some one aspect of
the total situation, by the compelling urgency of social conflicts, by the disclosures of aesthetic appreciation, by the
procedures and achievements of science, by man's moral

[2] Carl Becker, *The Heavenly City of the Eighteenth-Century Philosophers*
(New Haven, 1932), p. 6.

and religious history and experience. Somewhere, too, in all this will be found the philosopher's initial vision, colored by his own individual temperament and training, molded by some tradition of which he is the spokesman and vehicle.

It is factors such as these, pertaining to the currents of life preceding and surrounding each individual thinker, which contribute to the formation of philosophies and metaphysics. These factors do not readily appear in front of the philosopher in the shape of evidence and grounds to which he appeals for support of his beliefs. Yet they determine and color the kind of mind which he brings to the scrutiny of evidence. They show themselves in the choice of the problems which he regards as crucial. They weight the scales in favor of evidence and considerations of some one specific kind rather than of some other. What seems to one philosopher of paramount significance, eliciting a sense of wonder that the world should disclose just that aspect, will be taken in stride by another philosopher as needing little notice or comment. This whole situation here indicated is denoted by a number of terms, having the prefix "pre-": premise, presupposition, prepossession, prejudgment, and prejudice, the last named being applied only to the beliefs of those with whom we disagree. The term "perspective" is currently employed to remind us that whatever one sees, whatever one acknowledges, recognizes, and records is viewed from some specific, local vantage point, just one of many which are possible.

All of this comes to a head and finds its most crucial illustration in the major diversities of philosophical interpretations within metaphysics. The very allocation of these diversities and conflicts, the specification of what is taken to be the basic issue, an indication of the place where the shoe pinches most, expresses some temper and drive in the mind of the philosopher antecedent to the situation confronting him. I shall betray my own bias when I single out as crucial the broad issue vaguely indicated by the contrast between the philosophies embraced under the rubric of naturalism and those types of philosophy defined negatively in terms of a rejection of the premises and conclusions of naturalism. Neglect for the moment any rigorous inventory of the ingredients and contours of these contrasted types of philosophy. At the moment, let the names speak for themselves. I suppose the crux of the issue to lie in the interpretation and appraisal of whatever it is that belongs to man as man, and to man's life. Not life, of course, as the biologist uses the term, but life of which the poet speaks, when he says "how good is man's life, the mere living." It is life, conjoined with experience, comprising what is sometimes called the "human spirit," for which, in general, I shall use the term "mind," that is here in question; together with the relations which this domain sustains to that which men have called "nature." The philosophical battle lines are here confused and shifting, but that there is here a metaphysical shoe which pinches, and that it is incumbent upon philosophy to do what it can about it, is all too evident.

Now neither naturalist nor non-naturalist need, nor does he, deny any accredited fact either about nature or about man's mind. If one were content merely to record the facts, supplementing observed facts by facts inferred in accordance with the recognized canons of induction, there would be little occasion for any divergence. But which set of facts appears most provocative of wonder and to provide our best clue to an understanding of the total situation? If one is chiefly impressed by the episodic nature of man's life measured against its setting in nature's vast processes, by the continuity between human and prehuman life, by the panorama of physical nature as a "blindly running flux of disintegrating energy," one will say with Professor Becker that we must regard man as "little more than a chance deposit on the surface of the world, carelessly thrown up between two ice ages by the same forces that rust iron and ripen corn, a sentient organism endowed by some happy or unhappy accident with intelligence indeed, but with an intelligence that is conditioned by the very forces that it seeks to understand and to control." [3]

The question as to what in this statement is factual, a report of the available evidence; and what is not quite so factual, falling on the side, say, of the climate of opinion sustaining the thinking of Professor Becker—this question is not easy to answer. The statement just quoted is weighted with overtones of emphasis, interpretation, and implication, dictated by something other than the stark facts themselves. It is as if the writer said, "I give you the indubitable facts, but I will also suggest what they mean; they convey a hint to man not to lay too much emphasis on any unique achievements or possessions of man's life or of his mind. There is no dimension disclosed to us within man's experience which is incommensurable with the dimensions of nature's existence. It is wiser to interpret man's mind and spirit as but one of nature's many curious achievements or experiments."

On the other hand there are those who are chiefly impressed by the fact that the human mind has come to exist, to exhibit qualities and powers so strikingly discrepant from anything that nature has elsewhere brought forth. They are led to wonder whether the nature which has achieved the miracle of generating mind is quite the same

[3] Carl Becker, *op. cit.*, p. 14.

unaided nature as that which produced the solar system and the ice age. That consciousness should appear at all, that it should come to harbor the wealth of meanings and values there resident, that a being should develop capable of prizing truth and beauty and justice, this is the marvel beside which the careers of suns and planets pale into insignificance; all of this is the wonder.

This hint as to where the issue chiefly lies does not, I realize, take us very far; and the broad contours of naturalism and anti-naturalism but vaguely begin to take shape. There are depths and subtleties and variant strains in each of these two great philosophical types and traditions. The point is that they are philosophies. Each betrays some measure of initial preconceptions and directions of interest and emphasis, prior to the acknowledgment of objective facts and of the available evidence. No accredited fact need be neglected or denied by either type of philosophy. The fact that a brain lesion is accompanied by a disturbance or loss of the capacity for coherent thought or by a lapse into unconsciousness, together with a vast mass of equally well-attested facts—such facts demand acknowledgment by the idealist as well as by the materialist, by non-naturalist and naturalist. None of these diverse philosophical views affects the findings or the technique of the brain surgeon operating upon his patient. A philosophical interpretation of the total meaning of the empirical, observable findings is irrelevant to the task which he has in hand. As a philosopher, he may decide that the total relevant evidence points to the view that man's conscious life develops under the conditions imposed by body and brain but is not itself an adjective or a resultant of physical and biological processes. Or he may conclude that man's spirit is a name given to modes of behavior and structure which are as completely physical as anything found in nature throughout space and time. In either case, the laboratory and clinical findings remain what they are.

One further preliminary matter deserves notice. No one can fail to be sensible of the difference between the character of philosophical discussions and writings on the one hand, and the accredited exposition of scientific theory and knowledge on the other hand. The philosopher defends a position, he refutes opposing theories, he argues for the validity of some one comprehensive insight as over against its rivals. Philosophers fall into sects and schools, adhering to some specific tradition which they hope to keep alive; or they are reformers, initiators and founders of new movements. I would avoid drawing the lines too sharply here. But surely there is nothing quite comparable in philosophy, morals, or metaphysics to the contents of a college textbook in physics or calculus. All physicists and mathematicians will agree substantially with the theories and formulations contained therein. This area of common agreement does, indeed, shade off into an outer fringe of more doubtful and disputed matters. Both the foundations and the ultimate implications of physics and mathematics are less assured and agreed upon than the large middle area of tested facts and accredited theories. It is this settled middle territory that appears to be lacking in philosophy and metaphysics. It gets squeezed out between the objects of the philosopher's preoccupation: between foundations and implications, basic premises and synoptic comprehension. It is an understandable pathos which finds expression in the wistful longing that the issues of philosophy might be amenable to the procedures of science, that philosophical conflicts could be assuaged if philosophers would only adopt the methods of scientific inquiry. There is nothing, it is said, inherent in the nature of scientific inquiry which restricts it to any special type of subject matter and thereby limits its competence and adequacy as the proper instrument of man's entire intellectual activity, directed upon the acquisition of knowledge.

The sciences which offer the maximum degree of fundamental agreement are those which are concerned with non-human things and events. They are, first of all, the physical sciences: astronomy, physics, chemistry, and geology. The middle territory of assured matter of fact and verified hypotheses lying between initial presuppositions (if any) and ultimate implications is, in these sciences, the most extensive of any. The biological sciences are a close second in this respect. In bacteriology, anatomy, physiology, and biochemistry, conflicting schools and partisian "isms" are hardly more in evidence than in the physical sciences.

It is when we come to that intellectual activity concerned with understanding the life of man, his history, his mind, his experience, that the picture changes. There is here no dearth of acknowledged matter of fact. Indeed, there are almost too many facts, so many and of such overwhelmingly diverse natures as to lend support to differing and conflicting perspectives and interpretations. Both the initial premises and prepossessions and the meanings and implications borne by the facts encroach much further upon the middle area of acknowledged matter of fact than in the case of the physical and biological sciences. The assured and accredited facts are less decisive for the determination of an adequate theory of the nature and meaning of man's own life. The vast discrepancy between man's mastery and understanding of physical nature, including animal bodies, and his tragic failure to understand and to order his own life, stares us in the face. It is again understandable that this failure should be ascribed to our unwillingness or inability to use the methods which have proved so successful in taming the forces of physical nature, in order to achieve a comparable degree of success in the domain of human life and living. It is plausible to say that the barrier to this achievement is to be looked for in the assumption that there is that in the nature and endowment of man's life and mind which sets them apart from the realm—call it "nature"—which lends itself to theoretical and practical mastery by means of the accredited procedures of scientific activity. And this brings us back, by a circuitous route, to the spectator view of knowing.

If knowing is the activity of a spectator, then the attainment of knowledge signalizes the existence in man of that which has withdrawn and extricated itself from the nexus of interactions in which life is caught up. The mind's bondage to determinants such as the climate of opinion, and to the fortuitous contingencies of time, space, and history, presents itself as an obstacle to be overcome. This is the intent of knowing. For the fruition of this intent, man may have embarked upon a venture which, being man, he can never carry through to completion. "Men must know," remarked Bacon, "that in the theater of human life, it is reserved for Gods and angels to be lookers on." If this be true, then the quest for knowledge is on all fours with man's quest, say, for justice and for peace; yet men do pursue them.

The root of all dualities and tensions between knowing and doing, between knowledge and life, lies in the nature of the intent characteristic of each side of these dualities. If you want to know things for what they are, do not let your knowing introduce any changes in the things to be known. That is the intent of all knowing. The intent of practice, of all practical arts and doing, is to make things different, better, more suitable, more useful and satisfactory. No agent, but only a spectator can fulfill the intent of knowing. With this radical and primary difference, other far-reaching diversities are associated. Life and actions center around and stem from a vital center, an individual organism, body, mind, or self. This is a thick center, loaded with its interests, drives, and active tendencies. These serve to discriminate and give attention only to those features of the environment which are of concern to it. Life is partial and selective. The world which comes within the horizon defined by its interests, is *its* world, and *its* world is not *the* world. For life and action there is no one world which is *the* world. There are many worlds, each defined by and carved out of the one world. But life knows nothing of that one world. To recognize it, to go from *my* world to *the* world, through, it may be, *your* world, requires an intent and interest radically divergent from any that life can supply. It requires a withdrawal from life, impartiality, catholicity, and disinterestedness. Only a spectator can achieve these or even understand the claims which they make.

The horizon which spreads out before a spectator has dimensions which are closed to life and action. All that lies within the past has already been achieved and enacted. No change may be made in it. It lies outside the range of practical interests. All that can be done with the past is to view it as a spectator, in memory, imagination, and historical reconstruction. But the reconstruction transpires in the present, in the mind and judgments of the historian. The past is untouched by anything which we may now do. I cannot now decide to have done something in the past.

I can wish that I had, but such wishing conveys no knowledge of the past.

Again, life and practice require action, and action requires decisiveness. It is exigent, and brooks no such suspense of judgment until all the evidence is in, as does the cognitive and theoretical attitude. Only a spectator, relieved of the necessity of action, can afford the luxury of waiting, withdrawing, and suspending judgment. All theories are subject to incessant revision. There is no undoing of practical actions and of the decisions that lead to them.

Now all of these recognizable traits which we ascribe to man's intent to know, his pursuit of knowledge, amplify and illustrate what it means to assume the attitude of a spectator, in contrast with that of one consonant with life and action. The perspective provided by life and the satisfaction of its needs and wants become subject to a radical transformation in the pursuit and acquistion of knowledge. There is a reversal of the direction of the demand vector. Instead of demands made *by* the organism *upon* its world, knowledge asks that demands made *upon* the mind *by* things be acknowledged. The only interest now admissible is the interest in suppressing all interests save that of being a neutral, disinterested spectator. This disinterested interest runs athwart every vital and practical interest. The pursuit of knowledge, the intent of the activity of knowing, is more than just one additional interest, another facet in the complex congeries of drives which comprise the stuff and substance of living. It is tangential to all the vital and practical interests of men, the spokesman of a new dimension, introducing into man's life a kind of tension and duality, spoiling the innocence and finality of experience itself.

The spectator of a Greek drama was a θεωρός, whence our word "theory." Language bears witness to the intimate connection, if not fusion, between knowing and seeing. To see is to believe, if not to know. Vision is the most intellectual of the senses, and, if Elliot Smith be right, it was the extraordinary development of the organ of vision in man's mammalian ancestors which prepared the way for the growth of all his intellectual powers.

The linguistic identification of vision and cognition was established long before men had any understanding of the physical and bodily processes involved in the act of seeing. It was taken for granted that the eyes were transparent windows through which the seer, mind, or self looked out upon the world. There it was, just waiting to be seen. There was no thought of any active interchange or complicated transaction involved in just seeing things. When it was discovered that light had a finite velocity, that the eye and in particular the retina was not translucent but opaque, this account of vision as something simple and direct had to be abandoned. Eye and brain are energy receptors, transmitters and transformers. They are implicated within nature's transactions. It becomes difficult to imagine how any aspect or function of vision can be withdrawn from this nexus of interactions. There is no place here for any detached spectator. This is a small-scale paradigm of what appears to have happened along the entire front, when any organ and function of cognition is explored. Are not all men's beliefs and ideas the deposit and resultant of innumerable transactions which compel them to forefeit any claim to disinterestedness and detachment?

The principle of indeterminacy in physics has been employed to clinch the indictment of the spectator. A good spectator ought not to distort or dislocate that which he sees. He ought to catch it as it is at the moment when he sees it. But a minute object moving at high speed, say an electron, has to be hit by a bullet of light in order to become visible. This gives it a shove and prevents our seeing or measuring its actual position. Electrons are like politicians. Turn the light of publicity upon them and they no longer behave as they did in the dark. It looks as if nature had conspired to prevent our seeing what she is, or was before we turned our gaze upon her. Nature expects us to act and to interact, not to stand aside and contemplate her from any detached vantage point.

Indeed, was it not for the requirements of life, the successful maintenance of life's energies and the satisfaction of the needs of life, that nature endowed animals with sense organs? This was early surmised by Malebranche and Descartes, and Sir Oliver Lodge remarked that our senses were developed by the struggle for existence and not for the purpose of aiding scientific inquiry or obtaining philosophical insight. To be sure, some information about the lay of the land, some hint of approaching danger or the presence of food, is requisite for the business of living. But such information is keyed to the specific needs and demands of the organism. It is partial, selective, and biased. It is furnished with none of the flair for impartiality, catholicity, and disinterestedness which characterizes the cognitive interest. It does not issue in the discovery of *the* world which is other than *my* world.

Physics and biology have planted sensory functions, sensations, and perceptions within the nexus of nature's events and transactions. Anthropology, history, and the social sciences have done the same for men's ideas and persuasions. These too are generated at the crossroads of interacting tracks of happenings and energies, the interplay and conflict of vital interests from which there is no escape. What is called knowing is, within the perspective supplied by these sciences, a phase or incident within the processes of culture and history, just as are fighting and lawmaking. Knowing is one specific function, differing in any way that may be supposed from all other specific functions. But its own function is not to be defined in a manner which requires that it be the activity of anything which stands outside of the concourse of transactions and interactions which comprise the stuff of history and of life.

Is there any cognitive function which can still be viewed as the activity of a spectator? There is still one citadel to which the spectator can retreat. It is one from which he has sallied forth to achieve some of his greatest successes in the field of the sciences. The most elementary form of this is the activity of counting. Counting is an activity in which nothing is done to the things counted. There is no active interference, no give and take between counting and things counted, as there apparently is in the relation between seeing and things seen. If, in seeking to know how many chairs there are in this room, my act of counting shoved the number up or down, as the act of seeing is said to give a shove to the electron, I would indeed be badly off. The number system, in terms of which I report the results of my counting, is conventional and arbitrary, a matter of custom and convenience. Twenty-three chairs in the decimal system are thirty-two chairs in the septimal system. But, however reported, the number is known for what it is, independently of anything I do. Indeed, I do not do anything with the chairs at all. This absence and elimination of interaction is just what is meant by being a spectator. It does not mean just blank staring. I engage in an activity, that of counting, without, as an agent, doing anything to the objects counted.

Now this activity of counting and the mathematical apparatus and procedures which have grown out of counting are of such great importance because they point to one type of entity in nature which is capable of being known as by a spectator, whose knowing does not interact or tamper with what is thereby known. Such entities are the numerical relations between physical particles and events. Such knowledge is compatible with the lack of any knowledge about the intrinsic nature of the items themselves. A knowledge of relational structures, expressed in terms of a mathematics which has developed from simple counting, has vindicated the spectator idea of our knowledge within the physical sciences. In relativity physics, the interval between two events in the four-dimensional continuum is the same for all observers no matter where they may be stationed or what their relative motion may be. Different observers will allocate the space and time aspects of the two events in differing ways, depending upon their own relative motion. Relations, relational structures, intervals, correlations, and statistical probabilities are what remain as knowable by a neutral, disinterested spectator whose cognitive activity does not modify what he knows.

There is another aspect of scientific knowing, especially in modern science, which is often cited as having completely vanquished the spectator idea. Science is experimental. An experiment is a doing and a making. It is a practical art. Of course it is; but it needs at once to be added that such practical manipulating and contriving is a preparation for and is instrumental to an activity in which the experiment terminates, the activity of standing aside and observ-

ing as a spectator. The Principe Expedition in 1917 carried
through a sustained experiment to determine the bending
of light rays from a star field as they pass the sun. What
prodigious technical skill and practical planning went into
the making of that expedition! But the culminating and
dramatic moment came when the photographic plates were
developed and the tense observers became spectators of
what they saw on the plates. Nor were they troubled at that
time by any doubts as to the authenticity and objectivity
of what they then saw, arising from their knowledge that
vision involves the distortion and dislocation of what is
seen. At that moment they ceased engaging in the practical
art of experimenting. They became spectators. Something
akin to experiment and manipulation is preliminary to
all observation. One has to turn the head and focus the
eyes to see anything clearly. One has to make a microscope
and adjust it—experiment with it—in order to observe
what is on the slide. The experiment is performed for the
sake of the seeing.

The recognition that the knowledge of existence, accredited as scientific, depends throughout upon observation
is a tacit avowal that knowing is, in intent, the activity of
a spectator. The field of scientific knowledge is the totality
of existence brought within the observer's perspective. It
is the observer's perspective within which there is evidence,
the verification of hypotheses and predictions. The knowledge acquired by the procedures recognized as scientific
requires an observer who is, as such, a spectator. This is
but to say that the activity of knowing intends to be the
activity of discovery, not of contriving, manipulating, or
making things. Knowledge is not action. When a geologist
offers a hypothesis or theory as to how some rock formation
has come to be what it is, he takes it for granted that, in

so far as his account is correct, such and such a sequence of events in nature is what a competent spectator would have observed, had one been present. The mind of the geologist is a surrogate for such a hypothetical spectator. This is simply both the realism of our common sense and one which provides the tacit assumption of the sciences.

Throughout I have been taking the scientist at his word, when he insists that scientific knowledge arises in response to what the evidence demands and to nothing else. All evidence, as the world indicates, falls within the observer's perspective. Hypotheses and theories owe no allegiance to any arbitrary pressures operating from behind. These are to be escaped from and discounted just so far as possible. Whether there are any significant ideal demands, any requirements of theoretical intelligibility which may rightfully guide any one in search of knowledge, demands of a different order from any which come from the evidence, is not now in question. That there are such seems to me clear, and I shall return to this later. For the present, our interest lies in existence as it gets presented within the perspective of an observer.

For the history of the sciences is the story of the expansion of the field brought within the observer's perspective. Astronomy is the earliest science. The journeyings of planets and constellations are remote from man. They lie far beyond any horizon that his practical actions can reach or touch. They can only be observed and not tampered with. As the sciences grow and proliferate, man the observer annexes more and more territory to the field of observation. The observer's perspective widens. Regions not so remote as the stars, lying close to man, are added and fitted into the framework of observation. They thereby become suitable territory for scientific attack and exploitation, for all the procedures of observation, for the construction of hypotheses concerning the ways in which observed items hang together and are correlated, for verification, prediction, and subsequent control. For this is the road which leads to practical mastery, to the technologies and practical arts founded upon man's observation of correlations in space and time.

Finally, at long last, man himself and all that pertains to his life and his career become swept within the observer's perspective. The development of the sciences pertaining to man—anthropology and history, psychology and the social sciences—comprise the final chapters in the story of the expansion of the observer's perspective. That perspective brooks no setting of any boundaries to the field of observation. All the provinces of existence have been corralled within one world, to be known and mastered by the techniques of observation. This one world asks for a name, so that we may designate it and realize that it is one world and that all existence knowable in this manner is comprised within it; there are two names which offer themselves, and which men widely use: "nature" and "experience." And the logic of the entire development here outlined makes it easy, if not inevitable, that these should be taken as two names for the same thing, for this one world which is embraced within the observer's perspective when that perspective has expanded to its utmost limits. Experience and nature, empiricism and naturalism coalesce.

In this expansion of the observer's perspective, which is the growth of the sciences, what becomes of the observer himself? It is man the observer who has created all the sciences. The observer surely exists. There he is, experimenting, observing, constructing hypotheses, examining the evidence, carrying on all of the theoretical activities requisite for the acquisition of scientific knowledge. Not only these cognitive activities, but all the activities in which man engages, all of his life and living, ask that they too become known in the same manner. They ask for an observer, so that they may be brought within the observer's perspective. What happens, then, to the observer himself? Why, the answer lies open before us in the history of science. The observer disappears, as observer. This is, I take it, what Lewis refers to when he speaks of the flight from the subjective which has accompanied the entire development of science, not only the physical sciences, but all sciences. The Astronomer Royal for Scotland has just this in mind when he tells us that "science is knowledge when the observer is infinitely remote." [4] Being off at infinity, he may be disregarded, so that once more everything comes within the field of observation, inclusive, factual, and objective. The sciences proceed apace on just these premises. Philosophy has picked up the trail and in our time has made extraordinary and ingenious efforts to locate within this one world not only man the observer, but all of his life, his mind, and his consciousness; it has thereby sought to annul any disparity or duality between mind and nature or between man's conscious life and the fabric which is housed by nature—a duality which has become stereotyped in the space metaphor of "inner" and "outer."

Does any of the knowledge yielded by the procedures pertinent to the observer's perspective, thus become global and single, meet the stipulations implicit in the Socratic demand that man should have such knowledge as would illumine all the ranges of his life, and does it enable him to live in the light of what he may discern as the good? The detachment and withdrawal from action contemplated by the Greek thinkers was for the sake of such discernment. This

[4] Ralph Allen Sampson, *Science and Reality* (London, 1928), p. 76.

spectator has now become the observer, sweeping all existence into one observable order, himself vanishing to an
infinite distance to reappear only as a specific set of items
and relations observed and inferred. In this world there is
an inexhaustable profusion of happenings, of concomitan-
cies and sequences, and discoverable correlations amongst
them. But in principle that is all. To push this cognitive
venture to its uttermost limits is the vocation of the sciences.
It is not self-evident that the knowledge thus acquired will
avail man in determining the ends at which he should aim,
or in deciding upon the principles in terms of which his life
and action shall be organized.

That the cognitive activity which is science needs to be
interpreted within the context of something more comprehensive, is recognized in all quarters. Is this wider context
that of life and experience, as something which just transpires and is enacted, something which men have, undergo,
and enjoy; or is this wider context itself a vehicle of knowledge, of a kind not provided within the observer's prospective? Some duality and contrast there is, in either case. The
nature which he observes, even when that nature has been
expanded to include himself, is not the experience which he
enacts and enjoys. Does this life and experience itself disclose an order and dimension of existence disparate from
any which gets within the observer's perspective? Or shall
we, with Hume, leave life and experience autonomous and
masterless, utilizing what may be known within the observer's perspective, but not itself subject to any criticism
or appraisal which knowledge may yield? The answer
hinges upon what we are to make of the relations between
man's life and experience, and that nature which is the
correlate of man the observer. For if knowledge, of the
order exemplified in all the sciences, is based upon ob-

servation, as it is, then the nature which such knowledge discloses is *that* nature which is the correlate of man the observer. It is *that* nature which is open to man the observer. To specify it as *that* nature, carries the implication that there is some other nature, and that *nature* may be ambivalent. We are on the threshold of dualities, contrasts, and tensions with which man's metaphysics has attempted to deal, and to his metaphysics we have now to turn.

CHAPTER II

Man's Metaphysical Sense

PHILOSOPHY IS NOT SCIENCE NOR IS IT life. Nor is it some third thing entirely different from either of these, untouched by the procedures and achievements of science and by the exigencies and commitments of our actual living. It shares with science the spirit of detachment and disinterested inquiry, and it shares with life the sense of urgency and concern. It seeks to envisage the nature of things in the widest possible perspective. But the scene which it would embrace and understand includes more than the things and events which present themselves within the observer's perspective when the observer has succeeded in discounting himself and in retreating to infinity. That which is comprised within the observer's perspective does not exhaust existence. Not only man the observer, but man engaged in all the activities of his life and experience is there to be understood as best we may. Man is immersed and caught up in the currents of his life and history, and there is no escape from these as long as he is to live and to act. These, too, philosophy would understand and comprehend. Reflective thinking, which is philosophy, is stationed within life; it is integral to man's experience. At the same time it is the scrutiny and estimate of the total venture of living, such as may be achieved only by a spectator.

There is paradox here, not dissimilar to that contained

in the injunction of St. Augustine that it is the vocation of the Christian to live within the world yet not be of it. But our paradox is somewhat more terrestrial and it has a wider sweep. The quality of speculative detachment, interfused with the warmth and immediacy of life, pertains not only to philosophy. It is the prerogative of all experience and life on any level which is typically human.

There is good authority for doubting the wisdom or the success of trying to serve two masters, and there are those who see in this double allegiance of philosophy both to knowledge and to life the source of its confusions and failures. Let philosophy ally itself with one side or the other. Either it should throw in its lot unreservedly with the sciences, modeling all its pronouncements upon the techniques of scientific observation, hypothesis-making, and testing, and thereby make good its claim to supply us with knowledge; or it should express and give articulate utterance to the meanings latent within human strivings and enjoyments without adding to our authentic knowledge. It may express in prose what the poet utters in imagery and metaphor.

Everyone knows that the term "metaphysics" is a linguistic accident. Had the editors of Aristotle's writings placed his work on First Principles before his book on Physics we should, presumably, talk about "prophysics" rather than metaphysics. The Greek preposition μετά carries not only the meaning of "after"; it also means "beyond." It refers to a territory off at a distance beyond the boundaries which circumscribe the region with which we are more familiar and which is more accessible. This double meaning of the Greek preposition was, in a way, fortunate. It was well that a term should be forged which did have this connotation of "beyond." For metaphysics, in the European tradition,

evinces a concern for some area or dimension of being
which in some sense does lie beyond some other area with
which it is contrasted. Man's recognition of some such fundamental contrast is the prime ingredient of what I shall
call his metaphysical sense. I want to indicate some of the
forms which this has assumed and some of the problems
to which it has given rise. I shall want to ask among other
things whether man's metaphysical sense is itself an adventitious historical accident, foisted upon men's thinking
by local and provincial circumstances or even, as has been
surmised, by the linguistic structure of Greek grammar.
I shall want, eventually, to ask what man's metaphysical
sense will make of the contrast between man's life and the
habitat within which it is lived.

The metaphysics of Plato was, without doubt, a two-
world theory. There is the sensible, phenomenal world,
and there is the world of intelligible Forms. This duality
is reflected in the contrast between the functions and organs
employed in the apprehension of what belongs to these two
dimensions. Sense experience is set over against reason.
There is a corresponding duality and tension within man's
moral experience. The contrast between these two dimensions, a duality pertaining both to existence and to man's nature, has very much to do with that duality of life and knowledge, of practical activity and theoretical knowing, of which
some account has already been given. Here are, throughout, contrasts, dualities, and tensions, and Plato's metaphysics springs from a sensitiveness to their far-reaching
range and their import. The epithet "two-world" theory is,
however, misleading if it is taken to mean that the two
worlds are separate and fall apart. Plato certainly did not
so intend. The terms μίμησις and μέθεξις, imitation and par-
ticipation, are evidence of Plato's belief that the two dimen-

sions and worlds do not fall completely asunder. Each bears, in some manner, upon the other. A sense of fundamental contrasts, never to be erased, a sensitiveness to the tensions which they generate, together with an unwillingness to let them become stereotyped in a frozen dualism—these motives delineate the genius of Plato's metaphysics.

The metaphysics of Aristotle does not, I think, show so wide a departure from that of his master as is sometimes supposed. To apply the term "naturalism" to the metaphysics of Aristotle runs the risk of overlooking that strain in his thinking which is a continuation and development of the Platonic dualities. He criticizes Plato for his inability to overcome the separateness of the two dimensions of existence, but the sense of contrast and duality, the metaphysical sense, is far from being obliterated. The duality of matter and form, of motion and the unmoved mover, of change and the changeless, pervade his physics, his ethics, and his metaphysics.

Christian theology was more than a translation of the metaphysics of Plato and Aristotle into a different language, transposing it into a key consonant with the energies of a religion which had captured men's minds, but it was at least this: It, too, envisaged two dimensions, two worlds. The drama of man's life and of cosmic history centers around the contrast between the *Civitas terrena* and the *Civitas Dei*. The settled order of medieval life and thought, both the feudal structure of society and the *Summa* of St. Thomas, are deployed against a background pervaded by a haunting sense of the profound and awful contrast of the two poles between which man's fate is suspended.

These are the ancient and traditional dualities, with which Greek, Christian, and medieval metaphysics undertook to make their reckoning and to settle their accounts.

In these traditions, the emphasis falls on the duality and contrast between two orders and dimensions of existence. These are, in a sense, "two-world" theories; both worlds are there, objective, rooted in the texture of things. It is with reference to the emphasis upon this, that a recent lecturer, not himself a professional philosopher, but a student of literature, has remarked that "briefly and broadly, the issue is what it has always been and always will be, the age long issue between naturalism and super-naturalism." [1]

To define the issue solely in terms of the contrast between two worlds, nature and supernature, may tempt us to overlook one aspect of the situation which was never absent in these older traditions, and which has pushed itself into the foreground in all or most modern metaphysics. If there are two contrasted dimensions of being, both there, pertaining to the nature of things, this objective duality can mean nothing for man's life unless it finds an echo, a recognition and response in his own life and experience. The objective categories of Greek metaphysics, such as *being* and *becoming*, will press for a translation into the language of experience. This is one of the reasons why, by and large, the issues of metaphysics have come to be pivoted around the category of experience rather than the older categories of being and becoming. There are other reasons for this shift, which will concern us later. It is this category of experience which justifies us in speaking of *man's* metaphysical sense as a human possession, an ingredient of his life and experience. It is as empirical as his aesthetic sense, his moral sense, and his common sense. How we are to understand this category of experience, what it contains and what it may exclude, lies ahead. One thing at least is evident and must be said at once. The categorial shift of

[1] W. M. Dixon, *The Human Situation* (New York, 1937), p. 22.

emphasis to which reference has been made carried with it, initially, a continuation and a deepening of the sense of duality and contrast. It consisted in a redirection of man's metaphysical sense rather than in any weakening or annulment of it. In fastening upon all that becomes enacted within man's life and experience, he became aware, more acutely than ever before, of the duality of his own experience and the circumambient order of things within which his experience is set. When we moderns think or speak of dualities and dualisms, of contrasts, which are the source of metaphysical problems and perplexities, it is the duality of experience and nature, of mind and nature, or spirit and nature, which is primarily intended. The revolt against dualism means for us the revolt against this metaphysical contrast.

It is a mistake, I think, to view this duality as entirely modern. It was certainly not absent from the older metaphysical formulations of the Greek thinkers. Platonic ideas were indeed objective forms, to be discovered in the supersensible and, in one sense, supernatural order. But man's soul is the principle of his own life and thought. For the Greek thinkers, the contrast between the possessions and principles of man's life and mind and their cosmic environment was, in many ways, overshadowed by the contrast between two objective dimensions of things there in the world, but it was certainly not lacking. It may nevertheless be said that the metaphysical sense has, in response to the impact of many complex forces within the modern age, come increasingly to signify a preoccupation with and a sensitivity to that one outstanding duality which has become telescoped within the contrast of spirit and nature, and which has come to be, in so much modern philosophy, the paramount issue.

Whatever shape it may have taken and in whatever language it may have found expression, man's metaphysical sense, his apprehension of far-flung contrasts and tensions, is a perennial accompaniment of his reflective thinking. That this is the case is indicated by the linguistic form which philosophical and metaphysical problems and discussions commonly assume. They are, quite generally, formulated in terms of a conjunction which conceals or betrays a disjunction. Something and something else is the stereotyped formula for innumerable books and essays in philosophy. Change and permanence, the temporal and the eternal, process and structure, matter and form, convention and nature, existence and essence, the one and the many, appearance and reality, the actual and the possible, the particular and the universal, terms and relations, abstract and concrete, experience and reason, data and their interpretation, subject and object, mind and body, God and the world, the real and the ideal, the right and the good—such as these are the perennial contrasts which have supplied philosophy with its staple problems. Not all of them receive equal attention in any one epoch of intellectual history, or in the thinking of any individual philosopher. Some one of these great dualities will stand out as having a maximum sweep and urgency. To penetrate its meaning and nature will be thought to illumine all the others. Taken in their totality and viewed in the perspective of history, they cannot but leave in our minds the impression that something of far-reaching moment is uncovered in man's recognition of these dualities within and between his experience and his world. They give evidence of man's tacit acknowledgment that his life and his world pertain, not to one single dimension, but to two, and that man is what he was called by Sir Thomas Browne, the "great amphibium."

Man's Metaphysical Sense

There can be little doubt of the historic kinship of man's metaphysical sense and that which has found expression in his religions. That religion is definable in terms of some radical duality and contrast and of the implications of such dualities for man's life, with all the ensuing tensions and the resolution of these tensions, seems, in the light of history, to be evident. Many of the shapes which these dualities have assumed in the history of religion can evoke only pity and revulsion. They have joined hands with many dark and sinister forces in man's strange historical career. Religious beliefs and practices are bathed in both darkness and light. But throughout, a profound sense of the contrast between the levels on which life may be lived and organized, evoked and accompanied by a sense of some metaphysical duality, has been the earmark of the historical religions. It is borne in upon man that he dare not stabilize his life in terms of the familiar, the obvious, the near at hand. He is not to put all his eggs in one basket.

If we view man's metaphysical sense as an awareness of and concern for primordial contrasts and dualities in the world and in experience, we shall need to answer the question as to what distinguishes those contrasts which evoke the metaphysical sense and those which do not. Why turn over to metaphysics a concern for certain contrasts when we are content to leave to zoology the difference between whales and starfish? We meet with differences and resemblances wherever we look. The world and man's experience contain an unending variety of kinds, types, and of individual entities. What we come upon anywhere is some difference between this and that. So-called metaphysical contrasts may mark off from each other larger areas, more inclusive types, but one wonders whether there can be any intrinsic distinction between two types of difference, or

ne coming within the jurisdiction of common
science, the other of metaphysics.

is question, What is the difference, if any, between
ysical contrast and one which has no particular
ical bearing, is itself a metaphysical question.
And in the history of metaphysics there is discernible a
strain and tension between two interests and motives. On
the one hand, Aristotle invites us to consider and to survey
the nature of existence as such. "There is a science," he
says, "which investigates existence as existence and whatever belongs to existence as such." Existence is the one
universal and comprehensive trait in which all things share,
and metaphysics is the science which fastens upon an elucidation and clarification of what it means to exist. The
insight gained in this way will yield no information as to
what particular things exist, as to the structure of atoms
or the concrete happenings of history. Nevertheless, that
a penetrating analysis of the meaning of existence as such
yields more than a stark reiteration of the bare fact of existence and being, is shown both by Aristotle and by other
philosophers of the first order. The query as to what it
means to exist is not to be answered by enumerating the
contents of existence, the things that have existence.

On the other hand, in exploring what it means to exist,
metaphysics has, from time to time, found it necessary
to say that there is more than one meaning of the verb
"to be," more than one way of existing. There are different
modalities of existence, different and contrasted dimensions of being, such that if any entity is to enjoy existence
it has, as it were, to conform to the requirements of the
modality and dimension to which it belongs. The differences and contrasts between two entities or areas, both
of which fall within one dimension of existence, are of a

different kind from the contrast between two modalities of existence. The notion that there are such different modalities of existence is certainly not lacking in the metaphysics of Plato and Aristotle. It is more prominent in Plato. Being and becoming, change and the changeless, are different exemplifications of what it means to exist. The meaning of existence is not the same as one goes from one dimension to another. Such contrasts are metaphysical. Nevertheless, for Aristotle, the first of these two motives enjoys a primacy. His central concern is with the elucidation of the meaning of existence as such.

If all of this sounds artificial and bookish to many of us, as it does, it is because we are likely to take it for granted that existence is existence and there is nothing else to say. We are likely to assume that everything that exists satisfies one and only one set of criteria, and that all existence falls within one dimension, such as nature or experience. The deliquescence of the metaphysical sense has proceeded apace within our modern climate of opinion. Man's sense of large-scale, significant contrasts, his metaphysical sense, becomes articulate in a metaphysical theory which recognizes that there are different ways of existing and which explores the nature of existence in these different modalities and dimensions. The dualities and tensions thus recognized may stiffen into stark dualisms. But they need not do so. Different and contrasted modalities of existence sustain relations between them. Such relations will differ from relations which hold between entities belonging to the same dimension.

These are very abstract statements. They acquire thickness when they are brought to bear upon the crucial issues which concern the adequacy of any one domain of existence to be the matrix within which everything lies, everything which is of concern to man and which is neither illusory nor fictitious. If nature is initially defined as the totality of existence, then any metaphysics which allocates different areas of being within the inclusive domain of "nature" will be "naturalistic." When, in this way, such philosophies as those of Aristotle and Spinoza are described as naturalistic, not very much has been gained. These philosophies are sustained by a sense of some type of profound and significant contrast between the order of events and existences in space-time, and a dimension of reality which is supertemporal and supersensible. The "nature" which embraces all that pertains to the mind and spirit of man does not coincide with the realm of existence which the term "nature" denotes. The inclusive use of this term but serves to blur the problematic contrast and tension of which man's metaphysical sense is the spokesman and the witness. Man's metaphysical sense is no strange aberration, a possession of some few odd and eccentric individuals. It is a persistent trait of man as he is, as characteristic of him as his sense of rhythm or his delight in drama. It is not factitious, a residue of artifice and convention. It is native to human experience, akin to natural piety. It is pre-reflective, antedating any explicit metaphysical theories, as language precedes grammar, and practical "craftsmanship" the theory of techniques. Thought and reflection have to clarify and deepen its deliverances and its insight. They do not engender, *de novo,* man's apprehension of significant metaphysical contrasts.

It is a mistake to suppose that man's metaphysical sense is episodic and parochial, an ephemeral interlude, or a preparation for something more solid, lucid, and reliable, so that it may be expected to bequeath its title to a worthier and more authentic claimant. It is a mistake to suppose that the metaphysical sense which became articulate in Greek

philosophy was provincial and local, due to the historical
circumstances and conventions of Greek culture and society.
It is a mistake to suppose that Plato's two-world theory was
an epitome and rationalization of the cleavage between
social classes, with contrasted economic status and function.
To be sure, the particular form assumed at any one time and
place by this metaphysical sense will show the impact of
all manner of variable factors and determinants. All of the
endowments of man's nature live in time. It is a mistake
to expect or to hope that man's metaphysical sense would
wither away if man could succeed in banishing from his
world all preventable misery, sordidness, and conflict, and
surround himself with satisfying objects. Man's metaphysical sense is neither evanescent nor illusory. It is a perennial
human drive, fraught with pathos and urgency. Like religion, it has been the source of endless fumblings and
humbug. But man would be less than human were it lost
or obliterated. There are, to be sure, regions and levels of
activities and experience where the metaphysical sense is in
abeyance and properly so. Were it present in full vigor, it
would be an intruder, upsetting the economy of our doing
and our enjoyment. When one is trying to find out why
one's car does not start, no metaphysical sense will be of any
avail. Technical skill and practical intelligence are called
for. And when driving is resumed, the interplay of habit
and alertness, the enjoyment of the open country, planning
what to do upon arrival at one's destination—here, too,
the metaphysical sense is in abeyance. There is so much of
man's living which follows the pattern of which such activities as these are typical. The everyday routine of life,
organized in the grooves made by recurrent wants, needs,
and enjoyments, our vocations and avocations, suggest
little or nothing which is touched by anything which could

be called a metaphysical sense. There is a primary stabilization of experience, in terms of what is familiar and reliable. Here are our common human joys and disappointments, our hopes, plans, and fears, deployed upon the undeniable things and occasions which comprise the web and warp of our common life. It requires, it seems, no metaphysical sense to enjoy the play and laughter of children, to take things as they come with good humor or resignation, and to utilize the resources proffered by our world to enhance the zest for life, and to multiply its satisfactions. This stabilization of our living is one of the chief meanings of common sense. Common sense is the organization of life in terms of the familiar and the reliable. Common sense accepts, at their face value, human wants and desires, as they come to life in the concrete occasions of experience. It accepts the things and circumstances with which we become acquainted through sensory experience, as things to be acknowledged and also to be utilized and exploited in the service of our needs and wants. The common-sense world, with respect both to the values around which its interests center and to the range of things which are there to be reckoned with and known, is a *surface* world. The term "surface" need carry no hint whatever of disparagement. The familiar, the reliable, and the readily accessible must lie near at hand and on the surface. To discern what, if anything, lies somewhat beyond the horizon of the near-at-hand requires that one detach himself from the exigencies in which he is implicated, and that he survey the situation as a spectator. Such withdrawal is needed to call forth a recognition of what may lie beyond and beneath, and to sustain the awareness of significant contrast which is man's metaphysical sense. Thus, expressed in whatever language and in whatever context it may be, varying with intellectual climate and culture, one primary metaphysical contrast is that between the readily accessible, the obvious, the face which things present to us, and some area or dimensions in the background, beneath the surface, characterized by some different modality of being. The other side of the moon is hidden from us, but that does not make it anything metaphysical. It belongs to the same space-time modality of existence as does the side which we see. Being observable, it is part of the phenomenal manifold. The recognition of its existence implies no disparity of a kind which evokes and sustains the sense of pervasive contrast and duality.

But there is another ingredient and drive within man's metaphysical sense. It is one which itself stands over in contrast with the recognition of dualities and tensions. This other phase of man's metaphysical sense is so prominent and compelling that it is commonly taken to define its essential characteristic. Metaphysics is taken to be above all else a search for unity, for some primal stuff, some one principle within which the totality of existence may be embraced, some single inclusive whole which shall render intelligible and coherent all the diversities and contrasts which things present. Metaphysics embarks upon the search for that which will restore the continuity and integrity of things which, at first, wear the aspect of abrupt discontinuities, dualities and contrasts. There can be no doubt about the role which this persistent search for unity, inclusiveness, and continuity has played in man's metaphysical thinking. But what have we here, save evidence of the way in which the metaphysical sense of significant contrasts has invaded metaphysics itself? Since Plato, the European metaphysical tradition in its full vigor has been carried along by the tension arising from the acknowledgment of significant contrasts and the effort to envisage these dualities in the light of some one organizing principle. It has never been content to allow these dualities to freeze into stark dualisms, nor to annul them. It is possible, I suspect, that the metaphysical tradition of other cultures, of ancient India, say, has a different story to tell.

There is one way in which this demand for unity, which is one half of the metaphysical impulse, has been met, which it will be instructive to note. Confronted by pervasive contrasts and dualities as we are, haunted by a sense of the tensions which they generate, one of the courses which we may adopt is to envisage the inclusive totality of things in terms of categories which are definitive of either one of the two contrasted areas. The characteristics of one domain, standing over against its other, are spread over the total realm of being, and in this manner is the duality apparently overcome and assuaged. That half of the metaphysical drive which is the demand for unity drowns out the other half, the sustained sense of significant contrast and duality. The direction which philosophy takes when it thus envisages the whole of things in terms drained off from one side of a pervasive, metaphysical contrast, may be called, borrowing and adapting Whitehead's phrase, the fallacy of misplaced inclusiveness and finality.

We are not unfamiliar with the havoc which the analogue of this fallacy has wrought in man's world. We have seen what happens when men fanatically devote themselves to a contingent, partial and historical institutional structure as if it were something absolute, inclusive, and final. If Hegel viewed the Prussian monarchy as the final embodiment of the absolute idea, he was guilty of this fallacy. He had failed to sustain the sense of significant contrast. This freezing of what ought to be inclusive and final in terms of what is but one of two, of many, breeds fanaticism and pride. It obliterates man's sensitivity to and tolerance of other and contrasted forms of life and society. It is understandable that men should suppose the remedy to lie in in renouncing any idea of inclusiveness, unity, and finality, and accepting, as if they were themselves final, the relativities, contrasts, and contingencies which life and history present. This is an analogy not too remote, in the moral sphere, to that fallacy of misplaced finality and inclusiveness with which our theoretical philosophy is also threatened. A philosophy which invests the inclusive whole of things with traits drawn from one side of a global, significant contrast commits this fallacy of misplaced finality and inclusiveness.

A sense of the disparity and incommensurability of man's own life and the world which surrounds him has, I have noted, never been wholly absent from his common sense and his reflective thinking. This will present itself as a metaphysical contrast and as a theme for man's metaphysics in so far as two dimensions of existence, two different modalities of being, are here in evidence. What it means to exist is revealed differently in man's awareness of his own life and being, and in his recognition of the manifold of events and relations which are comprised within the observer's perspective. It is in keeping with good linguistic usage to denote these two contrasted areas of existence by the terms "experience" and "nature." It is with reference to this fundamental contrast that the fallacy of misplaced inclusiveness and finality needs especially to be kept in mind. Neither experience nor nature is fitted to perform the office assigned to them by many current and widely prevalent tendencies of philosophical thought.

Take first the concept of experience. Initially, without any doubt, the term stands for something limited and specific, a definite kind of entity. It is not found everywhere. It exists, as I shall later on say, only where some mind or self lives through its experiences. It is characterized by a modality and dimension of existence which stands over against other modalities. It is not as dependent on space as are physical things and events. It is deployed in the dimensions of time in ways which mark it off from happenings which we ascribe to nature. There is conscious enjoyment in experience, none beyond experience, and there are vast stretches of existence lying beyond experience. The area of experience is also stereotyped over against the domain of thought and reason. The antithesis of empiricism and rationalism presumably means something. Experience denotes a quality of immediacy, of warmth and intimacy, of actual presence, which marks it off from all that lies at a distance. To experience a pain is quite different from remembering one, or thinking of pains suffered by others but not felt in any actual experience. These statements require amplification and justification, and wait a further clarification of what it is that the term "experience" denotes. The essential thing at present is the fact that experience falls on one side of a profound, significant contrast. It is man's sensitivity to contrasts such as this which evokes and sustains his metaphysical thinking.

In view of these contrasts, where experience is set over against something which is not experience, it is, I think, unwise and misleading to employ the term "experience" to denote a single inclusive area, holding within itself all diversities, all problems, all with which men are in any wise engaged and concerned. So to do is to run the risk of endowing the areas in contrast with which experience is defined with traits and characteristics which they do not deserve or own. It is to commit the fallacy of misplaced inclusive-

ness. Idealists, such as Bradley and Royce, expose themselves to this fallacy. For them, the only dimension and
modality of existence is that possessed by experience. There
is nothing which transcends experience; nothing remains
with which it is contrasted. As such, the sense of significant
contrast is not sustained, and half of man's metaphysical
sense is in abeyance. To be sure, it comes to life again in
disclosing tensions and dualities within experience, between finite and limited experience and absolute experience. But the damage has, I think, already been done, in
using a term whose significance depends upon its contrast
with something else to denote an area inclusive of *all* contrasts.

The realm of existence denoted by the term "nature"
has had fluctuating boundaries, specifiable in terms of that
with which nature was contrasted. One such contrast was
that between the natural and the supernatural. To have
achieved a sense of this contrast, to have marked off a
domain safe from the intrusion of anything uncanny, dis-
rupting the orderly rhythm of observable processes, was a
signal achievement in man's intellectual history. Through
this and other routes, the broad lineaments and contours,
the defining categories of what it means to exist within the
dimension of nature, became relatively fixed and stable.
Nature is the domain of whatever exists and transpires
within the dimensions of space and time. Φύσις became the
subject matter of physics. The natural sciences are those
which are concerned with the things, happenings, and relations, discernible or inferable within the matrix supplied
by space and time. This is the physical nature which is prior
to and contrasted with our apprehension of nature, our
enjoyment and exploitation of nature, our human experience of nature. Nature is the object of our interest and

concern. That nature is set over against us, observable and usable by us, but not inclusive of us and of all that is an ingredient of our experience.

These are the overtones with which the meaning of nature has been invested. This contrast arouses the metaphysical sense. It is problematic and challenging. Over against nature is spirit, and what are we to make of their contrast and of the relations in which they stand to one another? Such relations there surely are, and that part of man's metaphysical sense which is his quest for unity and inclusiveness comes into play. Now to characterize this one total domain as nature, in the light of the meanings, with which this term is loaded, can hardly be a happy choice. The philosophies which do this fall a prey to the fallacy of misplaced inclusiveness and finality. I doubt whether a term thus stamped with the impress of significant contrasts is fitted to perform the function assigned to it. Neither experience nor nature can sustain the burden thus imposed upon them. All of this is very much more than a matter of words, a quarrel as to which word it is best to employ. It is a question as to what things are and may be known to be. It concerns the dimensions and modalities of existence.

There is another reason why the realm designated as "nature" is taken to be the candidate best suited to cover the entire range of existence. We need a domain which is, in principle, accessible to our minds and to our knowledge. If it should lie beyond all possible ranges of knowledge then there is nothing further, or nothing at all, which is to be said about it. That the possibility of knowing depends upon the ability to attain a kind of detachment, to assume a spectator attitude, has already been said. More will have to be said about it presently. But it, too, is subject to the hazards of misplaced finality. All of the knowledge which we denominate as science is based upon observation. Observations supply the test of hypotheses. We manipulate and experiment in order, ultimately, to observe. The activity and attitude of the observer is present throughout. As such, it exemplifies the spectator idea. But the observations which issue in any knowledge which we are willing to call scientific have one characteristic. The observer has to eliminate himself. He has to recede to a distance, ideally, as the Astronomer Royal has said, to an infinite distance. Now if we suppose that the spectator idea and ideal of what knowing is or should be, is entirely realized by such an observer, that all knowledge is exemplified by the sciences, one has, I think, another example of the fallacy of misplaced finality.

The canons which prescribe the rules and set the frame of reference for the acquisition of such knowledge as falls under the rubric of science operate as the solvent of metaphysical contrasts and dualities. All existence that may be known, in accordance with these canons, falls within one world of observed, observable, and inferable matter of fact. All existing matter of fact, all knowable structures, qualities, relations, and happenings are comprised within the one framework supplied by space and time. What other name can we give this one world but "nature"? Hume has Philo refer to that "vague indeterminate word 'nature' to which the vulgar refer everything." This propensity of the vulgar, when refined, clarified, and given free rein, becomes the premise of a philosophy for which nature is the inclusive totality. Man, the observer, seeks to lodge every existing and knowable entity within the one order of space-time nature. Himself, as observer, he must eliminate. But himself, as observer, in receding to infinity, will now reappear as a set of items or relations within the field of

observation. Something happens here analogous to the
reappearance, on the other side, as one branch of a hyper-
bola of one half of an ellipse, as the eccentricity of the conic
increases. The more scientific and less metaphysical psychology becomes, the more does it locate the mind within
the nexus of nature's events. That is where everything is
to find lodgment. But man, the observer, is not the whole
man. There is the entire range of his experience, his strivings, and his enjoyments, the life which he enacts and lives.
That, too, he would understand and comprehend for what
it is. Shall he then put his experience into nature, so he
can observe it, view it as a sequence of events within the
space-time continuum? As observer, this is just what he will
do, and has done with ever-expanding success. He will do
this in order to be able to predict and bring under control
the phenomena which may be anywhere presented. There
is no thought or suggestion here of questioning the enor-
mous importance of pursuing this observation of phenomena as far as may be, in the interests of practical mastery
and predictive control, and of keeping the total area thus
observed free from the intrusion of metaphysical echoes.
Science is a cognitive enterprise with limited liability. The
energies of man's own life and experience, observed as
events which happen, as phenomena, no longer have the
status which they have as ingredients of his own life and
experience. Man is content neither with just having his
experiences, nor with inserting them as events into one observable world. He would understand his own life and
appraise the principles in terms of which it is and may be
organized. To become reflective, to be a spectator of the
modality of existence which experience exemplifies, is not
quite the same thing as being an observer of phenomena,
watching the panorama of events spread out in space and

time, formulating the results of its observations, experiments, and hypotheses in terms of functional correlations.

There is, however, one further aspect of this whole affair of knowing, whether as a reflective spectator of the life of the mind or as an observer of phenomena. It will take us back to man's metaphysical sense. For there is one contrast which runs through the entire gamut of man's encounter with his own life and with his world. It is both trivial and profound to speak of the tension and duality between what man has and what he wants. Among the things which man has are the gifts presented to him by the objects which he encounters in the course of his experience. We call these gifts data, the given. Being given to us, we have them. They are not man's only possessions, nor his most intimate. A great deal of philosophical analysis has played upon the nature of the given in man's experience. The given has, at times, been supposed to come to us in detached, separate bits, jumbled together and needing to be set in order by us, as in a jigsaw puzzle. At the other extreme, the given has been thought to be furnished us in a manner which requires that nothing shall be done with it but to accept it as it comes. It is, of course, the theoretical activity of knowing, not any practical interest, which is here in question. At one extreme, represented by a common interpretation of the Kantian analysis, the mind in knowing carries on a synthetic and organizing activity. At the other extreme, the mind in knowing stands for the bare fact of awareness, inert and translucent.

Now it might be thought that any interpretation of knowing as the act of a spectator assimilates, in principle, the cognitive attitude to the aesthetic attitude. What is given to us asks to be accepted and enjoyed as we find it. Neither in cognitive nor in aesthetic activity is anything done to the thing that is given to us for our observation, beholding, and enjoyment. To be sure, what is observed to be given, cognized for what it is, like the number of chairs in the room to be counted, may be the source of no aesthetic satisfaction. But, cognitively, I just have to be satisfied with the number that I find. There are six books there arranged thus and thus. I may rearrange them to suit me better and add or take some away. But that is a practical and not a cognitive activity. Knowledge means acceptance of the given for what it is observed and inspected to be. It may be aesthetically, practically, or morally as unsatisfactory as you please.

But something has been omitted in this account. Man's theoretical activity evinces also a theoretical dissatisfaction with what is given, a discontent which becomes enlisted in the pursuit of knowledge itself, and in the very activity of knowing. Solely in the interest of knowing the nature of things, there is a contrast and duality of what is given and what things ought to be if they are to provide cognitive satisfaction. The mind, engaged in the activity of knowing, refuses to submit to the given. There are theoretical and cognitive interests which impose demands upon the given. There are criteria and ideals of theoretical knowability and intelligibility.

It is, indeed, a strange paradox. All knowledge of existence requires that something be present as a gift and datum. This given is not to be tampered with, altered, or overlooked. There it is. It comes to us with an implicit demand that we recognize and acknowledge it, if we want authentic knowledge. I can abstain from the activity of knowing, just as I can shut my eyes. But when I open my eyes, I have to see what is there in front of me. I may not like what I see and I can set about to alter and improve it. And I may utilize and exploit what I find to serve my vital and practical interests. But to know what is there requires that I do none of these things. It demands the spectator attitude. And the surprising thing is that, just as a knower, I am not content with what I find and with what is given. The spectator idea is not thereby abandoned. Its fruition is postponed. There is so much to do before the mind can discover the kind of world which it will be willing to contemplate with intellectual satisfaction. But observe what it is to which we are committed if there are ideals of theoretical and cognitive intelligibility. The given must be accepted for what it is. You cannot alter "facts," if your intent is cognitive rather than practical. Yet the facts, the given, are not what you are willing to acquiesce in. Only one way is now open. You will be led to suppose or to point to the existence of an order and dimension of things, which does not coincide with the given. It is the existence of that order which will render intelligible the given. There is no manipulation or alteration of the given. That is left to the practical arts. Yet the given now acquires a character which, taken just by itself, as given, it did not possess. Some variant of the contrast, and the relation, between appearance and reality comes now to the front. It is man's metaphysical sense, a sense of the contrast between what is given and what would meet the requirements of theoretical ideals of intelligibility, the contrast between what man has and what he wants, which is here operative throughout.

The name which has been given to the seat and content of those ideals of intelligibility which are the source of our discontent with the given is Reason. This reason is not quite on all fours with animal intelligence, sagacity, and shrewdness. These are harnessed somewhat too closely to the service of practical ends, immersed so deeply within the nexus of vital transactions as hardly to permit the detachment and disinterestedness which pertain to the pursuit of knowledge. One may recall the distinction drawn by Whitehead between the two reasons, the one asserting itself above the world, the one sharing reason with the Gods, the other with the foxes, the contrast between Plato and Ulysses.

I realize how vacuous and abstract is the bare statement that ideals of cognitive intelligibility and rationality have guided man's pursuit of knowledge, and that it is man's metaphysical sense which keeps alive this contrast and tension between the given and a dimension of being which would satisfy such ideals. To fill in the picture would send us to the long history of man's entire intellectual life, his pursuit of knowledge in both science and philosophy. Science itself has a twofold root. There are two versions of what science is or should be, depending upon which one of these two roots is taken to be primary and dominant. On the one hand, authentic scientific knowledge is equated with a description of observed and observable phenomena, of the coexistences and sequences of what is given to observation, filling in the gaps hypothetically with more of the same, so that the entire field is encompassed within a one-dimensional order. In so far as the activity of knowing is pursued in the interests of prediction, control, and practical mastery, what is needed is just such a description of the regularities of nature's sequences. When early man learned that he could produce fire by rubbing dry sticks together, he exhibited, in principle, everything which is required for this manner of knowing. He must have observed somewhere that friction is followed by heat. He must have entertained a hypothesis suggested by this observation. He puts his hypothesis to the test, and it works. He gets what he wants. For the purposes of prediction and control, everything is irrelevant except a knowledge of the ways in which spatio-temporal happenings coexist, follow each other and vary concomitantly with one another. A formulation and description of such space-time relations amongst observable phenomena with the widest possible scope of generality and with a maximum of exactitude is the goal of this aspect of scientific activity. It eventuates in the descriptive discovery of the functional correlations of phenomena and the relative rate of change of one variable with respect to others. In this version of science, the activity of knowing is ancillary to the vital and practical interests of living. It is inserted into the stream of life's activities, just as much as is walking or eating. Yet even here, this is not quite the case. For our primitive man must have paused long enough, and withdrawn sufficiently from the vital activities of eating and walking, to have noted, as an observer, that friction precedes heat. Such observation is the herald of a type of activity which is not just another kind of doing, like running and fighting. It is an activity and interest other than that of control and practical mastery.

There is the other root and version of the pursuit of science. In this account, what is sought for is something more than a description of the regularities of nature's sequences. The usual way of putting this is to say that one wants not only description but explanation. Not only the question *how,* but the question *why* is asked. One would like to discover that, whatever it may be, which would render understandable the observed and observable sequences and concomitances. One will say, with Sir Joseph Needham, that "the essential business of constructive science is to increase the intelligibility of the universe." [2] To say anything like this is to be aware of an essential contrast between the order

2 *Order and Life* (New Haven, 1936), p. 5.

of things observed, and some order of things other than that presented by given phenomena, a dimension which is required if one is to make sense of the observed and the observable. Man's metaphysical sense of duality and tension has, in this version, crept into the activity of scientific knowing.

It is fatuous for philosophy to say what the sciences ought to aim at. There can be no doubt, however, as to the dominant drift in modern thought of what both scientists and philosophers have said what scientific knowledge, in fact, is. It is knowledge descriptive of the coexistences, the sequences, the functional correlation of observed and verifiable items within one space-time dimension of existence. In the pursuit of this knowledge, metaphysical entities can play no role. Aristotelian forms, entelechies, prime movers, substance, organizing principles, and purposes which operate behind the scenes, belonging to a dimension other than that of the observable and the verifiable, have vanished from the repertoire of the sciences. Or have they? Does some echo of man's metaphysical sense still hover around the pursuit of science? Are Eddington's two tables, lodged respectively in two worlds, a legitimate reverberation of this metaphysical sense? Is the other table, that on which he is not writing and could not write, a *bona fide* inhabitant of a dimension of being set over in contrast with the dimension given to his observation, or is it but a name for discernible features and relations into which the perceived table may be analyzed? Are all alleged metaphysical entities but names and abbreviated symbols of strands and stretches belonging to one single dimension of being, to be called, indifferently, experience or nature?

The answer to these questions hinges upon the significance and validity to be attached to man's metaphysical sense. Within the entire orbit of the life of knowledge, it is the metaphysical sense which is responsible for man's theoretical discontent with the given. One wishes, wistfully, that if the knowledge which is scientific be equated with a descripitive formulation of functional correlations among given items, this avowal not be taken to imply that the whole intent and scope of man's pursuit of knowledge is thereby exhausted. No neat surgical incision can safely be made into the living tissues of man's theoretical activities in pursuit of knowledge. Division of labor is indispensable. By and large, the procedure of the sciences has been steadily moving in the direction indicated by the terms "empirical," "operational," and "pragmatic." But always in the background hovers the lure of those ideals of theoretical intelligibility which originate in man's sense of the contrast between what his world gives him and what he would like to uncover beyond the boundaries of the given and which will render it cognitively intelligible.

The discovery and explanation of the nature of these ideals, their mutual interplay, their organization, their exemplification in experience and in nature, falls to the lot of metaphysics. Such explanation is needed to clarify the meaning of intelligibility. I doubt if it is possible to bring them all under any single rubric, unless it be just reason itself. But reason has its own life and the currents of that life flow through more than any one channel. I would here single out one somewhat specific facet of intelligibility and cite it but as an illustration. Its exploration would take us far. Its formal title is necessity. Since Hume, it has been the orthodox doctrine of empiricism that there are no necessary relations anywhere, except in discourse and logic and mathematics. And the necessities here disclosed turn out to be either instances of identities and tautologies, or the expansion of these into implicative systems, through initial definitions and the manipulation of symbols. The relations between matters of fact exhibit neither this type of logical necessity nor any other kind of necessity. The relations observed to hold between matters of fact which are of primary concern are the relations of coexistence in space and sequence in time. To fasten upon the relations of resemblance and similarity sends us off on a false scent. That was the blind path taken by the natural science of the ancients. It promises no clue to an understanding of the executive order of nature, the order in which things exist in space, and happenings occur in time. Spatial and temporal relations among existences, holding between matters of fact, are what they happen to be. Anything can be next to anything else, and any event can be followed by any other event, in the economy of nature as observed. No item in this nature implies any of its associates in space and time. Implication is an affair wholly of discourse and of logic. This is what we have to content ourselves with, because this is all that is given us in what we observe and experience.

I think that this statement, which is essentially that of Hume, is right in so far as it is an account in all literalness of the cognitive situation as it exists within the observer's perspective. Nothing is observed except the fact that something exists along with something else, and that one event is followed by some other event. Whatever regularities, rhythms and repetitions there may be are just the ones that nature happens to exhibit. There are no necessary relations intrinsic to the phenomenal manifold which comes within the field of observation. As observers, we stand in the same relation to the phenomena observed that the prisoners in Plato's cave stand to the shadows which flit across the wall.

But take now a situation such as this. One reads a book devoted to the exposition and development of a theme printed on its title page. Suppose that the book is well written and does contain the explication of a central theme. The book is made up of chapters, paragraphs, sentences, words, letters. The analysis may be pushed further, but stop there. These ingredients of the book are strung along within the dimensions of space and, in the writing or reading of the book, in time as well. Here are items, say, *a, b, c, d,* and so forth, which have a space-time order. These items, together with their space-time relations, exhaust the book as observed. A graph might be plotted showing the functional correlations of these observed phenomena. Suppose, now, that the successive items as observed, do develop a theme, in such a manner as to make the book coherent and intelligible. In this case there would supervene upon the observed and inferred space-time relations a new kind of relation, bringing with it a kind of necessity. It is the theme which requires that at this place and time, just this thing be said, just these words be used. Neither the central theme nor the relations exhibited by its development belongs to the plain of observed matter of fact and the time-space relations holding between items and phenomena observed. They lie beyond and, metaphysically, behind the phenomena. It is they which give the book whatever sense it has and which render it intelligible. But they are simply not observed nor are they discovered by formulating any functional correlations among space-time items. They lie in another dimension. Reading and understanding a book is a metaphysical exercise.

I have no thought of here suggesting that all of nature is a book to be similarly understood. But if she is, that fact will not be disclosed to observation nor come within the purview of a science primarily concerned with the formulation of functional correlations and the verification of hypotheses based upon them. Its discovery would require a little stronger infusion of the metaphysical sense, an unwillingness to rest content with things as observed, the ideal of some kind of necessity which would make intelligible the space-time relations which are observed and inferred, and a sense of the heterogeneity and duality of the two dimensions and modalities with which we would then be concerned.

Hume's thesis that there are no necessary relations anywhere discernible between matters of fact is a transcript and report of what the observer's perspective embraces. Its acceptance has become a matter of course in statements of scientific methodology, of the meaning of causality based upon the procedures of scientific observation and inquiry which would attain the maximum of empirical warrant and the minimum of anything metaphysical. Necessary relations, banished from the observer's perspective, take up their abode in discourse, in the manipulation of equivalent symbols, in analytic statements and tautologies. We are witnessing something analogous to what happened in the early modern period when physical nature was stripped of secondary qualities, and these could find refuge only in mind. To accept as final the banishment from existence of all necessary relations is as devastating as was the total exclusion from nature of all secondary qualities. Dualities have congealed into dualisms. Neither by moving in this direction, nor by sweeping both sides of a significant, metaphysical contrast into a framework fetched exclusively from one side, has proven adequate. Man's metaphysical sense, ranging widely and freely, keeps alive his recognition of contrasts, dualities, and tensions. It will also warn him not to close in too soon upon the totality of existence, with categories derived from but half of existence. The persistent duality of man's experience and its habitat, of spirit and nature, may fruitfully be explored, within the context supplied by man's metaphysical sense; and to this contrast we now turn.

CHAPTER III

The Mind's Possessions

THAT THE CATEGORY OF EXPERIENCE has come to occupy a position of primacy and centrality in modern thought and life has been noted. It has, in many ways, displaced the categories of being and existence with which the metaphysics of the ancients was preoccupied. This shift in the pivotal center of metaphysical problems and reflection is indicative of many forces which have gone into the making of our modern culture and mentality. The meanings which attend the term "experience" are fluid, complex, and notoriously difficult to render articulate with any adequate precision. Experience is that to which all men attach supreme importance. It is that to which men appeal both for the guidance of their lives and for the sources of their knowledge. The appeal to experience, in some sense, is the prerogative not only of those philosophies which are commonly classified as empirical.

There are two broad directions in which the meaning and content of that which the term "experience" denotes are to be looked for. One path leads to a wholly neutral meaning, the other to a non-neutral, a quite specific meaning. In the first of these two meanings, experience is the modern equivalent of the notion of being or existence as such. The concept of being is neutral because it makes no prescription and sets no limits upon the content of existence, but with this proviso, that anything which is the content of existence, any existing entity, must satisfy the requirements of what it means to exist. That there are such requirements, implicit in the meaning of existence itself, is the premise of Greek metaphysics. If anything is to exist, or does exist, it must exemplify the universal traits inherent in the meaning of the verb "to be." Why has not modern metaphysics, or the metaphysics which bears the characteristic stamp of modernity, been content to continue this tradition? Why has it substituted experience for being or existence? Part of the answer lies, I think, in the presence of a kind of latent or suppressed premise in Greek metaphysics. The nature of existence, as such, which metaphysics is to explore, must in any case be something that men can get at, something which comes within the range of what men may inquire into, refer to, and talk about. Metaphysics is, at the very least, discourse about being and existence and, as such, these must have entered the realm of discourse. So much so that, in entering the universe of discourse, it has seemed to some that discourse has completely swallowed the subject matter of metaphysics, and that this has entirely become an affair of words, grammar, and syntax. In any case, the inquiry into existence presupposes that existence is accessible. The accessibility of being is the premise of metaphysical inquiry. It is the premise of all inquiry. Now the fact that being not only is, but is accessible—otherwise we could not talk about it—requires a term and a concept which bring this premise to the surface and make it explicit. This is just what the concept of experience does. In this meaning, experience is simply a name for accessibility. Now just as the meaning of the verb "to be" neither prescribes nor excludes any content of existence whatever, so this meaning of experience does not specify nor does it limit the nature and kind of entity which belongs to experience. It is utterly catholic, universal, and neutral. It signifies sheer accessibility itself. It calls attention, in a way in which the concept of being alone does not, to the fact that the only existence that can in any way concern us, the only *being* that we can dream about or talk about, is *being* that is, in some manner, accessible. Nor can there be, in this neutral meaning of experience, any restriction or limitation of the mode of accessibility. All that I touch and see, imagine and dream about, all that I may think and talk about, belongs to the realm of the accessible. They all belong to experience. Accessibility is not limited to that which is gotten at through sense experience. That which is not accessible in any manner whatever is the analogue of non-being, and it shares the same fate. The fact that we can frame the notion of non-being, talk about it, even deny its existence, shows that it is something, and has then its own mode of being. And whatever may be declared to lie wholly beyond the pale of any accessibility whatever—well, there it is and its non-accessibility is itself accessible.

This explicit uncovering of accessibility which this meaning of experience denotes is significant. It is a symptom of a shift in the center of gravity of men's life and their world. Accessibility carries an implication which being and existence do not. Accessibility requires a preposition, and existence, as such, does not. Accessibility, to whom or to what? The meaning of being and existence is complete without any such preposition. We moderns may ask, "Being for whom?" The Greeks did not ask this. Being was being. It needed no prepositional adjunct. When Kant and Hegel append a preposition to terms denoting existence, such as *Dinge an sich,* or being which is *an und für sich,* or being

which is *for* another, they are importing into the concept
of being a prepositional and relational quality, derived
from the sense of experience as accessibility.

This prepositional implication of accessibility conveys
a hint that the notion of experience is losing its complete
neutrality and lack of any specificity. It is beginning to be
tied down and anchored to a quite specific kind of entity.
It is being brought within a restricted and limited context. What that context is has already appeared in the
conjunction of the terms "life" and "experience," where
life is a syncopated form of the active participle, "living."
How natural and inevitable is this conjunction! There is
nothing strange in writing a book about the life and experience, or the life and adventures, of Tom Sawyer. Experience is now no longer the attribute of everything which
is in any way accessible to us, stars enormously remote in
space and time, the mythological inhabitants of Mt. Olym-
pus, the distribution of prime numbers, everything and
anything which comes within range of any of our powers.
Experience, in this second sense, is anchored, localized,
and centered.

There is an analogy between these two directions in
which the meaning of experience veers off, and the double
meaning which belongs to φῦσις, "nature," in the development of Greek thought. Φῦσις has another meaning, one
intimately associated with the idea of birth, growth, and
life. It is this idea of birth and coming to life which is caught
by the Latin *natura*, derived as it is from the stem which
signifies "to be born." Nature is the mother of all things.
In Greek thought, to be sure, φῦσις as growth was not as
localized, not an exclusive attribute of some things only,
as are life and experience, in our usage. The two meanings
of φῦσις were too closely united easily to permit this. All of

nature exhibits growth. The influence of early animism is still making itself felt. Here, then, is a meaning of experience vastly more restricted and localized than is that experience which is a synonym for accessibility. Experience becomes individualized. In this sense, the question, "Whose experience?" is inescapable. Experience in the first, neutral sense, is not the property of any one owner. It is there for anyone to have access to. It is coterminous with all of being, all of existence that is, with which we are in any manner concerned. And of that with which we have no concern whatever, of that which is inaccessible, there is nothing whatever to be thought or said. The second meaning of experience implies a contrast, and a duality, the most momentous, I think, of any which have evoked and sustained man's metaphysical sense. Stated in the simplest terms possible, it is the contrast between those entities which have experience and those which do not. This is a metaphysical contrast because it pertains not to any difference within a single modality of existence, but to two contrasted ways of existing.

There is a variant of the metaphysical attack upon the nature of existence, which is to be mentioned before we inquire further into the nature and significance of this contrast and duality. The method which this metaphysical variant employs is somewhat different from the path followed by Aristotle in seeking to lay bare the nature of existence as such. It is a little more empirical and inductive, in the customary sense of these terms. It starts off from the content of existence, from things and types of things which we encounter and come upon, and seeks to uncover what it is that they all share in common. What are the pervasive traits found in all the specific things which exist, is the form the question now assumes, rather than the form, What does it mean for anything to exist? The difference between these two ways of putting the question is not absolute, but they lead off in different directions. The first of these two ways lies a little closer to the procedures of the sciences, at the classificatory stage of scientific investigation. The second way, that to which in general Aristotle adhered, is more reflective and speculative, less inductive. Now there is one risk to which this first approach is subject, from which the second type of inquiry is exempt. It is the danger of what now commonly goes by the name of the fallacy of reductionism, or of "nothing but." Had Thales, in identifying the nature of all things as water or moisture, intended to say that earth and air, fire and smoke are nothing but moisture, he would have been guilty of this fallacy. But of course he was not. What saves him is a duality, and a metaphysical one, the duality between a pervasive substance which does not appear at the surface, and the various surface forms or appearances which this underlying substance assumes. If you decline to recognize any such duality, and if you want to avoid the fallacy of reduction, there is only one thing to do. Affirm that everything is just what it is and not another thing. The cognitive attack upon existence will now consist solely in an observation and formulation of the coexistences and sequences amongst observed items. Had the Greek thinkers restricted themselves to this endeavour, there would have been no metaphysics and, I think too, no science such as developed, say, from the atomistic hypothesis. That everything is just what it is and not another thing becomes, when translated into the language of experience, the maxim that everything is just what it is experienced as being, and nothing more or else besides. The nature of each experienced entity is exhausted in the experience of it. As a warning against the danger of reductionism, these formulations serve a purpose. They serve notice that the content of existence is infinitely varied, that each occasion and item of existence has its own unique, individual nature which is not to be explained away. But to accept all these rich diversities and contrasts as final and ultimate, about which there is nothing to do, cognitively and theoretically, except just to acknowledge them, would be the end not only of metaphysics but of a good half of science as well. It would be to commit the fallacy of misplaced finality. The mind's ideals of theoretical intelligibility impel it to search for that which will render things intelligible. All explanatory procedures have to steer a course between the Scylla of a radical empiricism or positivism, which bids us accept diversities as we find them, and the Charybdis of reductionism.

This has been mentioned because there is a risk, not unlike that of reductionism, which is run when metaphysical inquiry takes the form of ascertaining the pervasive features of all contents of existence. The risk is this. If there are contrasted dimensions of existence, if there is some area which has its own unique way of existing, then its characteristics will escape formulation in any view which is intended to set forth the traits found in all contents of existence. This risk is not so great when, as with Aristotle, one investigates what it means to exist. It may mean more than one single thing. That type of theory which seeks to envision the nature common to all *contents* of existence may be called a greatest-common-divisor type of metaphysics. The greatest common divisor of two relatively prime numbers is unity. The greatest common divisor of two contrasted and incommensurable contents of existence would be just existence itself. The greater the incommensurability, the thinner will be the greatest common divisor pertaining to both.

Pepper has, for instance, employed the concept of a root metaphor. Each root metaphor yields a world hypothesis. The procedure is not quite that of Aristotle. In stead of investigating what it means to exist, one looks around at the content of existence and fastens upon some one impressive and pervasive feature of things found. The fact that things are similar, the contiguity and impact of bodies, the fact of organization, the fact of contexual leadings—some one of these lies at the root of those world hypotheses which have proven to be fruitful and to have attained a high degree of adequacy. The root metaphor is the greatest common divisor of everything that exists. It is a metaphor or divisor which has a thickness and content beyond bare unity or existence. The successful development of any one of these world hypotheses depends upon the range of cosmic commensurables. Each one of these world hypotheses encounters, in the outer fringes of the range defined by its own root metaphor, an area which begins to be recalcitrant. It runs up against existences which are incommensurable with the greatest common divisor which determines its categories. It meets with situations which are relatively prime to the factors in terms of which its own thinking is carried on. Its categories tend to become strained when they are stretched beyond the commensurables to which they readily apply.

Hume put his finger on this perplexity. He has Philo say, "Can a conclusion, with any propriety, be transferred from parts to the whole? Does not the great disproportion bar all comparison and inference? From observing the growth of a hair, can we learn anything concerning the generation of a man?" [1] The relative adequacy of the great world hypotheses, their persistent recurrence in the history of ideas, is ample evidence that the answer to Philo's question is not a simple negative. Yet Philo's question persists. It needs always to be asked. For if it is the case that existence presents itself in more than one fundamental modality, a single root metaphor, fetched from one mode of existence, will betray its inadequacy when it is applied to some different modality. And philosophy has to keep its weather eye open, as the great philosophers have always done, to these significant contrasts and dualities which show themselves to be incommensurable. The greater the discrepancy and incommensurability, the less adequate will be a metaphysical theory of this greatest-common-divisor type. Now I think there is no greater disparity among the contents of existence, among existing entities, than that between those which do and those which do not possess experience. It is imperative, I think, that we remind ourselves how momentous this contrast is, and the first question to ask of any metaphysics is what it does with this duality. Experience is a possession incomparable with any sequence, congeries, or organization of items, or relations among things and events where there is no experience. An illustration may best serve to remind us how significant and momentous this contrast is.

A small low-pressure area in the South Pacific is born, migrates eastward as it grows and gathers momentum and, in a few days, bursts with full-fledged fury over the entire Pacific area, and there thins out and loses itself in the encompassing atmosphere. Here is an individual episode in nature, compacted of moving air masses, temperature changes, condensations of vapor, and electrical disturb-

[1] *Dialogues Concerning Natural Religion,* Pt. II.

ances, all presenting a pattern of events in space-time. But these moving energy transactions find no resonance in any experiences lived through by cloud and air. They do evoke experiences of hardship, suffering, and heroic toil in the workers who must keep trains running and the mountain passes open. The imaginative mind of a novelist, catching a sense of the human drama, will depict the course of the storm as if it, too, were a drama. He personifies the storm, naming it Maria. But the ingredients of the storm possess and live through no experiences as do the minds of men.

Contrast this with another migration. Masses of men, women, and children migrate westward from the arid dust bowl of Oklahoma. Here is a human storm. The economist or social scientist will now play the role of the meteorologist with respect to this social migration. Here are economic pressures, "lows" and "highs," a massive disequilibrium the stresses and strains of which cause upheavals and dislocations. But what a wealth of meaning is here over and above any observed or inferred events and behavior! Here are hopes and frustrations, anxieties and fears, retrospective memories and prospective longings, things precarious and insecure. Not one of these nouns or adjectives, or the meanings they denote, is applicable to cloud masses or movements, as viewed within the perspective of the observer. The novelist who depicts this human situation has no need of imagining it to be a drama or tragedy. That is what it actually is, because it is compacted of human experiences and actions consciously lived through. There is no meaning nor are there any values in moving air masses. There are motions in space and time, and redistributions of energy. The moving masses of men hold and incapsulate meanings and values, because here are minds, centers of conscious life and experience. Here, alone, are there any values, and any meanings as well.

There are some extraordinary ways in which the term "experience" has come to be used by both scientists and philosophers. I read in a book written by a professor of astrophysics that science at a certain stage "has a double task before it; it must correlate the experiences within each molecule, and also correlate the molecules with one another." [2] He goes on to speak of "each atomic experience in the molecule" and the way in which it is to be represented. I think it extraordinary that a physicist should use this language of a molecule while the scientific psychologist tends to draw away from speaking of the experience of man or rat, and to concern himself solely with observed behavior. Experience, consciously had and lived through, does not belong to the observer's perspective. Behavior, as a name for events and interactions in space and time, does. The psychologist uses language more appropriate to obtaining the knowledge sought for than does, in this case, the physicist.

The molecule has a complex internal structure. It participates in energy transactions with other molecules, and it behaves differently in various fields. All this is a matter of experimental observation, inference, and hypothesis. The observations, experiments, the forming and testing of hypotheses occur in the experience of the scientist. There is no evidence, certainly none accessible to the physicist, that the molecule ever experiences anything. Now the quality which renders the having of experience so momentous, which confers upon it a unique status and which makes it incommensurable with all ranges of existence where there is no experience, is the quality denoted by the adjective "con-

[2] Herbert Dingle, *Through Science to Philosophy* (Oxford, 1937), p. 97.

scious." The abstract noun "consciousness" designates the presence of this quality of experiencing. There is no more striking tendency in many recent writings in both philosophy and science than the willingness or eagerness freely to employ the category of experience, and a reluctance to use the terms "conscious" and "consciousness," as denoting something the nature of which can be expressed by no other term which is not itself a synonym of "being conscious." The distrust of consciousness, the belief that if it be admitted as something quite fundamental there will, in the end, be no way of escaping the disease of subjectivity, the belief that the approaches which open out to a common world in which men may cooperate and communicate will be closed, that men will be thrown back into a shadowy realm of phantasies, caprice, and waywardness where nothing substantial and significant is to be found—these beliefs and the temper to which they give expression are wholly understandable. They are the outcome of certain ways in which the notion of consciousness has been deployed and has developed in modern thought, some of which I am to consider. They are due, I shall say, to the failure to make a complete inventory of the ingredients of experience, of the mind's possessions. In doing this we shall need at the same time to see what it was, under the conditions of modern life, which brought the idea of consciousness so prominently to the front, and which made it, and still makes it, so indispensable and fundamental. The having and the living through experiences is the prerogative of a unique kind of existence, unique, when measured against the totality of all entities whatever, which exist, which undergo changes, which possess structure and organization, but which are, however, not in possession of experience.

The possessor of experience is a mind. There is mind

wherever anything is experienced by way of sensing, feeling, thinking, purposing, remembering, striving. In the absence of any manner or degree of such as these, there is no mind. Experience (in the second, not the first, neutral sense) is that which a mind possesses. To say that it is a mind which holds title to the possession of experience is a way of saying that experience, in the sense in which it is now being used, comprises a kind of system, a mode of organization, with its characteristic structure and relations. The ownership of experience by a mind need imply no more than this, nor need it signify any sort of absentee ownership.

In this chapter we shall be concerned with one kind or aspect of the mind's possessions: those which are most intimate, those which lie nearest to the owner, so to speak, those which are the immediate possessions of the mind. Our account will need to be supplemented by a report of another aspect of the mind's possessions, in the next chapter. The immediate possessions of the mind are, in any case, and in every instance, qualified by the adjective "conscious." I take consciousness to be indefinable. In the case of consciousness, or the quality of being conscious, indefinability means something different from the indefinability of the intrinsic nature of any quality whatever. For there is an important sense in which all qualities are indefinable. They cannot be described. The unique quality of this particular shade of blue, or of the taste of peppermint, cannot be conveyed by any definition. The terms used in description and definition are generic. Uniqueness slips through the meshes of all class terms and common nouns. Nevertheless, this particular shade of blue can be compared with other shades. It can be assigned a position in a series. It is not incomparable with other qualities, each one of which is intrinsically unique. Now nothing analogous to this is found in the case of consciousness. There is nothing with which to compare it. There is no common divisor, no generic determinable (except existence itself) which can make the transition from the absence to the presence of conscious experience analogous, say, to the gradual increase in complexity of organization in physical nature. It is in this drastic and radical sense that consciousness is indefinable.

The contrast between things which have experience and things which have not depends upon the presence or absence of this quality of being conscious. Is this statement about a discoverable feature of things a fact, is it a theory, or is it a definition? It is certainly not any nominal definition. It is a report of a situation forced upon me by what I find. It is more difficult to disentangle the ingredients of fact and theory. In the end, there are no facts accessible to man in any mode of accessibility which are brute facts, not invested with any shred of meaning, isolated from every context, bringing or demanding no interpretation. The interpretation, implicit or explicit, is a theory. Nevertheless, I have to reject the view, often put forward, that this radical duality and contrast between entities having experience and existences not in possession of experience is due entirely to certain theories which have appeared in comparatively recent times, say in the last few centuries. The implication is that the problems which cluster around this contrast are factitious and that they will fade away when these theories are replaced by more adequate ones.

It is, for instance, sometimes held that were it not for the development of mechanistic views of nature, the disparity between the domain of consciousness and a world contrasted with consciousness, a nature completely physical and material, would never have presented itself. The mechanistic account of physical nature drove secondary

qualities out of nature. They had to find lodgment somewhere, and so an inner world of consciousness was devised
to house them. Put secondary qualities back into nature,
and the necessity for a unique dimension of mental entities
within consciousness vanishes. Mechanistic views of nature in the seventeenth century did determine what was to
be allocated to mind and conscious experience and what
was to be left to physical nature. But such mechanistic
theories did not create the geographical pattern which provided men with the two dimensions of man's experience
and the world of nature, nor with the profound contrast
between them. Some recognition of this duality long ante-
dated the rise of mechanistic theories of nature. It is not a
local and provincial episode in man's intellectual history.
A long-range view of that history gives every evidence of
man's persistent awareness of the contrast between that
which comes to life and is enacted in the experience which
he owns, and a surrounding world devoid of such experience.

This contrast is blurred but it is not absent in the animism of early man. Some awareness of the discrepancy between his own life and the things in his world to be noted
and used was never wholly absent. In his practical arts he
confronted things to be manipulated in terms of their observed properties and mode of behavior. He could not even
have invested things in nature with an *anima,* unless he
had first been dimly aware of his own *anima,* his own life
and activity. In early animism, the duality is confused. It
is just as true to say that early man conceived the mode of
existence belonging to his own life and experience on the
analogy of physical things, as to say that he interpreted
physical things in terms of his own *anima.*

In the history of European thought, the first large-scale

clarification of the confusions of early animism was due to the Greeks. The "secular character of Ionian civilization" of which Burnet speaks favored the growth of science and, for the first time, made it possible to interrogate the world according to canons which we recognize as theoretic and scientific. Greek philosophy began with shrewd speculation, cosmologies, and world hypotheses concerning the nature of things of which, in general, man and his life are but one particular exemplification. It was Socrates who first clearly drew attention to the discrepancy between the life of man and the nature which surrounds him. Socrates was the first philosopher to see that the greatest common divisor of nature and of man's life would not make intelligible what is in greatest need of being understood, man himself and his experience. This is the landmark which divides pre-Socratic and Socratic philosophy. Are we entitled to say that Socrates thinks of man's life and experience as characterized by the possession of the unique quality of consciousness? Cassirer believes that we are. Others are more doubtful and warn us against reading into Socrates and his successors the language and ideas of a later age. But there can be no manner of doubt that Socrates made central the duality and incommensurability of that which man enacts and lives through in his own life, and that which he observes and discovers in the cosmic scene surrounding him.

We need a convenient term to designate the way of thinking which depends upon the recognition of this contrast, a sense of the uniqueness of man's life acting as a counterweight to a greatest common divisor mode of thinking. I propose to use the term "animism." It is not the animism set forth in Tyler's *Primitive Culture*. It is not, at present, an animism which would find mind in those stretches of nature, of physical nature where, both for our common sense and our science, there is no recognizable mind. It is an animism which expresses man's sense and recognition of how significant a thing it is that there are experiences through which he lives, a sense of the disparity between that which becomes enacted in his own life, and other existence where experience is lacking. The unforced association of life and experience makes it not inappropriate to employ a term derived from *anima* to denote just this. In this sense, the societies for the prevention of cruelty to children and animals, and the absence of any society for the prevention of cruelty to minerals, rests upon premises supplied by the animistic perspective. This distinction between children and minerals does not lie in any difference between the observed structure and behavior of children and minerals. This distinction would not be revealed in any observer's perspective. This animism is no transient episode in the history of man's thinking. It was not fastened upon his language and his thought by the demands of some metaphysical theory or some particular set of metaphysical categories. It has been there, in the offing, ever since the secular spirit of Ionia banished the ghosts of that different, early animism from the outer world of nature, and Socrates gave expression to the existence which man enjoys.

Something important does unquestionably happen to this perspective of animism as we cross the threshold of the modern period. The idea of the conscious life of the individual assumes a primacy and a centrality which it had not previously had. Consciousness becomes that which an individual indubitably has, the most immediate and compelling of all his possessions. That which is discoverable within his consciousness and nowhere else provides the foundation and starting point for all his knowledge. Dewey has remarked that "the idea that mind and consciousness are intrinsically individual did not even occur to anyone for much the greater part of human history." [3] If this be taken to mean that what I have called the animistic perspective, the sense of the disparity between what man finds his own life to be and all other existence, I am quite sure that the statement is inadequate. If it is taken to mean that in the last few hundred years there arose a heightened sense of the individual and the experience which is his own, of his mind and consciousness, the statement is true and significant. Descartes and Locke are there to show it. Theirs is a different accent from that, say, of Aristotle. "What we miss in Aristotle," remarks Ward, "is a clear recognition of what we now call consciousness as the central feature of all psychical acts." [4] We may miss it with or without regret, but there is no doubt about the fact. It is not that Aristotle is blind to the distinctive energies resident in man's life, that the animistic perspective is lacking. Socrates had seen to that. When Plato and Aristotle speak of the soul, would they have understood the question, had it been put to them, "Is the soul, then, conscious of the experiences which it undergoes and lives through; are any of the activities of which it is the principle *conscious* acts and activities?" I would hesitate to answer for them. But Descartes and Locke would have said that it was a silly question, because it is the nature of the soul to be a thinking substance and to be describable in no terms other than those which denote consciousness. "Consciousness makes everyone to be what he calls self," says Locke. And for Descartes, the individual's awareness of his own conscious life is the starting point of everything that may be said about man, God, or nature.

I have recounted these commonplaces for two reasons.

[3] John Dewey, *Freedom and Culture* (New York, 1939), p. 21.
[4] James Ward, *Psychological Principles* (Cambridge, 1920), p. 6.

First, they indicate how close was the association between making consciousness so pivotal and central, and the enhanced sense of the significance of the individual in the new world which was taking shape. It might be said that some better way should have been found for expressing men's revolt from authority and tradition, their desire for individual freedom and power, than to clothe this revolt in so problematic a concept as that of consciousness and of that conscious life, inner and individual, which is the individual's own most intimate possession. Should they not have foreseen and guarded against all the waywardness, the disease of subjectivism, the egocentric dilemma, the fruitless dialectic of the problem of knowledge, which the notion of consciousness was to leave as a heritage for subsequent philosophy? The fact remains that all of the mighty energies released by the development of modern individualism, and liberalism too, be it said, in economics, politics, morals, and religion, found their expression and their warrant in the concept of the inner, conscious life of the individual.

That this is so may be seen by glancing at the altered status of two concepts, that of the individual and that of nature, in the civilizations denoted by the terms "medieval" and "modern." In the Middle Ages the status of the individual, in idea and largely in practice, was that of an entity defined in terms of its relations, its context, and its function. The individual belonged to a class, his rights and duties were defined in terms of his position in a graded hierarchy. So far as his status in society was concerned he did not stand on his own feet. He had, to be sure, an individual soul, linking him to a transcendent order, but one which was irrelevant to his station and duties within society. The individual was thought of in relational and functional terms. Nature, too, was not exempt from an analogous feudal and hierarchical order. But the nature which medieval physics described was neither functional nor relational. It was throughout qualitative, composed of unique individual qualities, just those which are disclosed in our perceptions of nature. No one of these qualities was dependent upon its context, upon its relations to other qualities, for the possession of its own intrinsic nature. Now in the transition from medieval to modern, nature and man each underwent a revolution. The individual who was functional and relational in medieval society became autonomous, defined by something intrinsic to his own unique nature, and by his own possessions. But the nature which had been the domain of irreducible, unique, individual qualities now becomes functional and relational. Continuities, serial structures, functional correlations, and variations become the categories in terms of which nature is to be understood and mastered. This reversal in the respective roles of man and nature could not but powerfully reinforce men's sense of the incommensurability of their own individual being and the de-individualized framework of nature. How else could man's enhanced sense of his own individual powers and freedom become articulate, save in the language of consciousness? The animistic perspective and the observer's perspective become more sharply defined in contrast with each other than ever before.

There is a second reason why I have cited these familiar things about the themes which started modern philosophy off. Speaking of the philosophical development which runs from Descartes and Locke through Hegel, Woodbridge pointed out that a "single conception, namely the conception of the mind, with its related conception of consciousness, has given to the whole movement its significant character and its typical problems." [5] He, in common with others, believed that this movement had run its course and that it was fruitless to develop that theme any further. Around the turn of the century three American philosophers, James, Dewey, and Woodbridge, undertook a fundamental revision of the premises with which this movement started off, a revision of the nature and meaning of the thing called "consciousness."

I, too, share the belief that something went radically wrong with the path taken by this philosophical movement, and I want to indicate where I think some of the difficulty lay. It should, however, not be overlooked that whatever the errors of this movement may have been, they were due to the effort made by these modern philosophers to safeguard the integrity and autonomy of the new individual who had emerged from the breakup of feudalism. They undertook to do this by exploring and fortifying the animistic perspective with its emphasis upon the unique nature of what man is and has, over against the world of nature. They did this by making the conscious experience of the individual the one indispensable premise.

Over against the animistic perspective is the observer's perspective. The scientific achievements of the new age could never themselves have been attained were it not for that heightened sense of individual freedom and activity which found expression in the concept of the conscious activity of the individual. The new knowledge of nature rested upon the appeal made to individual experience, experiment, and observation, and to the devising of new mathematical instruments, which were the creations—or discoveries—of individual thinking and intellectual activity. The conscious life of the individual provided the me-

[5] F. J. E. Woodbridge, *Nature and Mind* (New York, 1937), p. 321

dium in which all this activity went on, and men were not oblivious of that fact. There they are, two perspectives stereotyped in sharp contrast with each other. In the one perspective, the conscious experience possessed and enjoyed by the individual is the dominant and ultimate thing. In the other perspective, all existence, including man's life and experience, belongs to the field of observation. Everything is there, accessible and objective.

Now one of the things that happened in the development of this theme of consciousness was that each of these two perspectives pressed upon the other, deflected it from its natural and logical course of development, and prevented it from fulfilling its legitimate function. Consider, first, the influence of the observer's perspective upon the animistic perspective, for which the concepts of consciousness and experience were paramount. In the observer's perspective, everything there, in existence, is something to be observed, even the observer himself. Everything is projected upon one plane, everything is spread out in a phenomenal manifold. When this perspective is grafted upon the animistic perspective, experience will denote that which is experienced, with all the emphasis falling on the passive participle. Experience denotes the presence to awareness (for some conscious awareness must remain) of items sensed, perceived, felt, imagined, and thought of. There slips out of experience that quality denoted by the active participle, experiencing. The activity of experiencing becomes the presence of things experienced and nothing else. For Locke, the generic name for all these objective entities, objective in the sense of that of which the mind is aware, is "idea." An idea is "whatsoever is the *object* of the understanding when a man thinks." Empiricism thus is loaded at the start with a phenomenalist interpretation of experience, as if the only thing the mind had to do was to observe phenomena. *There* is a feeling, *there* is a splash of color, *there* is a sound, *there* is a flash of lightning. The influence of the observer's perspective, of the phenomenalist interpretation of experience, is crucial and instructive in the case of the experience of activity. It is the case that activity is not an observed phenomenon of experience, as are colors and sounds. Nor is it the awareness of kinaesthetic sensations. In being aware of ourselves as active, as willing, and as desiring, we are learning what it means to exist as a mind. In the observer's perspective we learn what existence means in another modality of existence. This experience of ourselves as active is also accompanied by an awareness of that which supplements this immediate possession. It carries a meaning which provides a basis upon which the mind can build a structure of knowledge and life beyond the boundaries of its immediate possessions. But the immediate experience is there, though not as an observed phenomenon. When so regarded, as by Hume for instance, it is the observer's perspective masking in the guise of the animistic perspective, the sense of consciously living through the activities of our experiencings. Since everything which belongs to man's experience is now lodged *there,* in the world of objective entities, consciousness is on the verge of fading away, or becoming thought of as a selected group of items, neutral with respect to any quality of consciousness. Or it is viewed as a transparent film of mere awareness about which there is nothing further to be said.

The animistic perspective moved within the orbit of the observer's perspective and became deflected. What it means to exist as a subject, as the possessor of experience, as a mind and self, became relatively neglected as a result of this preoccupation with items experienced. As for Descartes, although he uses the term "consciousness" repeatedly, his chief concern throughout is with the existences which he supposes consciousness to disclose. Beyond the fact that consciousness reveals its own existence as the negation of space, there is little more to say about it. Its nature is entirely transparent to any one who is conscious. It is like a translucent plane with no depth or thickness to it. Both Descartes and Locke are preoccupied with the objects of which we are conscious. This is the way in which the observer's perspective exerted pressure upon the animistic perspective.

But the impact of the perspective of animism upon the observer's perspective proved even more disconcerting. The individual's conscious life is now the central thing. How can there be any object of conscious awareness or observation unless the object is brought within the field of consciousness, and becomes a constituent of the mind, one of its intimate possessions? Whatever one is in any way aware of, whatever is present to the mind, has to get within the mind, be absorbed and possessed by the mind. The current of subjectivism is in full flood. The confusion of the two perspectives issues in a phenomenalist, one-dimensional version of all experience which tampers with the autonomy of man's conscious activities, of all the experiencings which he enjoys, and a subjectivism which tampers with the objectivity and autonomy of the world of nature which surrounds man. Each perspective was hindered from fully developing the implication and meaning of its own logic.

The subjectivism which results from making all objects accessible to the mind into literal possessions of the mind, located in consciousness, has more than one analogue in ideas and beliefs in morals, economics, and politics. The individual had freed himself from the social fixities which had tied him to his feudal status. He had a new sense of a world to be won and made through his own activity and enterprise. He acquired an equally keen awareness of his right to possess all that was the fruit of his own activity. The belief, with respect to property, that a man may do what he will with his own because it is his own, is the moral equivalent of Locke's doctrine that the understanding hath no other objects but ideas, ideas which are the individual's own possessions, incorporated into the substance of his own mind. The doctrine that an individual has a right to that with which he has mixed his labor runs parallel with the doctrine that whatever a mind knows is its possession. Modern hedonism defines the good in terms of the possessions of experience which are the most immediate, which make no claim beyond the fact that they are possessed in actual feeling. What can have a better title to being the possessions of a mind than feelings, pleasurable and painful? To feel them is to have them. The good has no content, beyond the feelings possessed in immediate experience.

These, then, are some of the directions taken by the movement of which the initial premises were formulated and expressed by Descartes and Locke. The basic premise was the concept of consciousness, and the primacy and ultimacy of the conscious life of the individual. This, itself, was a translation of the persistent perspective of animism into a form consonant with the emergence of a new individual. In view of all the predicaments in which this entire movement became involved—the waywardness and isolation of a mind shut in behind walls with no windows, in possession of contents which it can neither share nor communicate—is it not the part of wisdom to give up the premises from which this entire development began, and start afresh? When consciousness is thus made pivotal and ultimate, when all of the mind's possessions are regarded as contents or states of consciousness, the material at our disposal is too flimsy, intermittent, and evanescent to construct out of it any stable structure whatever. The philosophers who have moved within this tradition have tried to do the impossible. To make consciousness ultimate drove them to say that all existence disclosed to consciousness vanished when the consciousness of it faded away. There are existences of which this is true. A feeling exists only while it is being felt. Its being felt is an affair of consciousness. When the consciousness of it ceases, the pain no longer exists. The existence of a mental entity is identical with the consciousness of that entity. But this must hold for any entity which is possessed in this manner by the mind. Whatever the mind possesses, the mind must be conscious of. When its consciousness vanishes, there is nothing for the mind to possess. Accessibility has become possession and possession means conscious awareness.

The ease and apparent inevitability of this procedure, once we accept the premise of consciousness, is indicated by some common forms of language. Consider the three statements: There is a book. I am seeing the book. I have a perception of the book. The first statement reports a fact. It announces the appearance and presence of the book out there in space. So far, there is no reference to any observer or reporter, least of all to any consciousness. Yet the book does not announce itself or report its presence. It is accessible to me, otherwise I could not announce its existence. And so one slips into the second form of statement, I am seeing or I see the book. There it is again, but the fact that it is the object or target of an act performed by me now becomes explicit. The act of seeing belongs to me, but not to the book. That is still out there. Accessibility has now become prepositional, and can be put in the passive form: the book out there is seen by me, is accessible to me. But the state of affairs indicated by this second proposition is unstable. If challenged to give some warrant for saying that it is a book which I see, I have to appeal to something in my actual possession. I shall now say, I have a perception of the book. Here is again a prepositional phrase, "of the book," but hasn't it become superfluous? All that I now am actually in possession of is the perception. I had better stick to what I have got and not take any chances. The prepositional phrase becomes an adjective qualifying my perception. I have a bookish perception. Like the pain, of which the existence coincides with the consciousness of it, the existence of the bookish perception is wholly dependent upon the consciousness of it. When I cease to be consciously aware of it, it ceases to exist. Accessibility has become complete possession. What havoc this makes, both of the world and of ourselves, all because we have this entity, consciousness! Were it not for that, the book would still be there.

When the question is asked, What then are the mind's immediate possessions, the experiences through which it consciously lives, and what role do they play in the economy of man's life, the answer is paradoxical. It points in two quite opposite directions and may teach us one or the other of two lessons. We may speak here of consciousness. On the one hand, consciousness is fleeting and evanescent, fluctuating along the scale from momentary brightness and intensity till it fades away and disappears. It comes and goes like a shadow world made of unsubstantial phantasms. When we drop off into a sound dreamless sleep, or go under an anaesthetic, it vanishes. When we wake in the morning it comes back. But even this language is not appropriate. Losing consciousness, in dreamless sleep, is not like losing something which remains hidden from us, but still existing, until we may again find it. When we lose consciousness, it is not lost; it goes out of existence and is annihilated, and when we wake, it is not that something lost has been restored to us, but a new creation is there, bursting in upon us from sheer nothingness. What nonsense this makes of our selves! Is my self annihilated each night, and recreated each morning? Nothing provided by consciousness can sustain the stability, continuity, and integrity of the self. And all the while, there is that which is subject to none of the hazards and predicaments of consciousness, something which is there when consciousness vanishes between sleep and waking. It is the body. The living body has a continuous existence from birth to death. It can do what consciousness cannot do, supply the self with an enduring structure, even be itself, in all of its functionings, that mind and self for which one looks in vain in the shadowy domain of consciousness.

If consciousness is so ill equipped to supply the stuff out of which a self may be built, it is no better fitted to sustain knowledge, or to implement the pursuit of knowledge. The presence of consciousness renders precarious the integrity of the world as known. It threatens to engulf and completely to possess the existence which we would seek to know. It transforms the solid substance of things into phantoms. Once this shadowy realm is disposed of, the book can still be there, in the world, and not vanish into an adjective of the mind's conscious possession. There is the book, the body sees it, and this is all.

No wonder that men should have a sense of how poor a thing is consciousness, how fragile and unsubstantial will be anything made from what it can offer, how little it has to contribute to the making of a self, or to sustaining any of the structures which man would build up, his knowledge, his arts, and all that belongs to the fabric of his human world.

But this is not quite all. There is another and a different thing to say about consciousness. In spite of all its evanescence and unsubstantiality, it is the only thing in our possession which provides the locus of whatever it may be which has value for us, and which is of concern to us. Were consciousness not to exist, there might be any amount or kind of other existence, matter say, but nothing whatever would matter. There would be no better or worse in a universe entirely devoid of sentience, of some mode of conscious life. In such a world, mindless and unconscious, it would not make the slightest difference what happened or what existed. Suppose that, on our planet, animal and human bodies would behave and go through all of the motions they now go through, but were completely and permanently anaesthetized. In these circumstances, nothing would make any difference, or be of any concern whatever. No values of any sort would have a foothold in such a world as this. So when the question is asked, What does this paltry, evanescent, and fleeting thing that men call consciousness, what role does this play and what does it amount to, the answer is, Everything that matters. The physiologist, Sherrington, puts this question and he answers: "All that counts in life. Desire, zest, truth, love, knowledge, values, and seeking metaphor to eke out expression, hell's depth and heaven's utmost height." It is so much that is done by so little.

The mind possesses the immediacies of all the conscious experiences which it undergoes and enjoys and through which it lives. Experience reveals a modality of existence incommensurable with all observed structures, events, and relations spread out in the dimensions of space and time. All of man's experience discloses to him what it means to be a mind and to have experience. In the observation and contemplation of everything objective, we are enjoying something immediately possessed in conscious experience. In the absence of these immediate possessions, there could be neither man's living nor his knowledge. But were these immediacies the mind's sole possessions, both life and knowledge would be poorer than they actually are. The mind has other possessions, and to these we have now to turn.

CHAPTER IV

The Mind's Meanings

IN WHAT HAS THUS FAR BEEN SAID IN THESE chapters the emphasis has been placed upon certain pervasive and significant contrasts and dualities such as those denoted by knowledge and life, spectator and agent, the perspective of animism and the observer's perspective, experience and nature. A sense of the significant tensions which pervade man's experience, and of which he becomes acutely aware when he reflects upon his life and the circumstances within which his experience is set, has been taken as the source of very much of man's metaphysics. One such contrast, with which we were concerned in the last chapter, is that between beings who possess experience, endowed with the capacity for living through experiences by way of feeling, enjoying, and suffering; knowing, striving, and willing, and, on the other hand, the vast, even infinite array of existences which do not have experience. Consciousness surely pertains to the former, but not to the latter.

The sense of this contrast cuts deeper than any statement to the effect that there are two kinds of phenomena, occurrences, which we come across and may inspect, mental phenomena with which we become acquainted through introspection, and non-mental, physical phenomena which we observe through the channels of sense experience. So to report the situation does scant justice to the scope of the contrasts and dualities which are here in question. In viewing man's conscious life as a chain or system of phenomena, even if they are labeled "mental," in one way places his mind on the same plane as that to which other phenomena belong. And where this is done, one is plagued with all the riddles as to the relation, whether that of parallelism, interaction, or identity, between two sets of phenomena so completely different, yet belonging to the same phenomenal plane. In the perspective of animism, experience is not so much the appearance and presentation of phenomena to be inspected, as it is the existence of that which is being enacted and lived through. Here there is life and action and experience, with the accent on the active participle, experienc*ing*, rather than on the passive participle, experienc*ed*. It has been noted that the conception of man's experience as the bare awareness of items which are there and presented is due to the encroachment of the observer's perspective upon the perspective of animism. But when the activities deployed in man's conscious experience, his actions and enactments, are made pivotal, when the animistic perspective is sustained, the resulting duality leaves us not with a single world but with two worlds, two perspectives, and there appears no way in which to translate the language of one perspective into that of the other.

All of these dualities, rifts, and contrasts in the texture of things and in man's experience are problematic and disconcerting. Men are loathe to accept as final a divided world. Half of man's metaphysical sense bids him search for continuity, unity, and an inclusive totality. These bifurcations have, in modern philosophy, found their most concentrated expression in the contrast between mind and nature, where the conscious life of the individual is taken to be the defining trait of mind. The centrality of the problem of consciousness in so much of modern philosophy gives utterance to a powerful sense of the role which the individual has assumed under the conditions of modern life. The emphasis upon the life of consciousness has lent definitiveness and depth to man's awareness of the contrast between his own life and the cosmic habitat in which that life is lived. The bifurcation between conscious life and physical nature, signalized by the Cartesian dualism of *res cogitans* and *res extensa,* set the stage for modern philosophy. To overcome this rift, to domesticate mind and consciousness within the world, playing fair with all the differences exhibited by mind and physical nature, without reducing either to the other, became a matter of primary concern both for philosophy and for life, and it still remains so.

In the early period of modern philosophy, mind could not be integrated within nature. It had to fall outside nature because nature was poor and impoverished. The secondary qualities had been taken from her. She was deprived of everything but motion, and her structure and behavior was thought to be fully capable of formulation in the laws of classical physics and mechanics. To put mind back into nature, to escape the necessity of regarding mind as a supernatural intruder, it became necessary to give back to nature all that she had been deprived of, and she had been deprived of much indeed. To bring mind and nature together was bound, then, to become one of the main concerns of philosophy, than which none is more urgent and pressing. What kind of a nature is it to which mind can be restored, so that the rift between the two can be overcome? Or will it be found that when nature has been given her full due, when all the secondary qualities, and the other ingredients of what men experience, perceive, and enjoy, are restored to nature, even then nature will not be quite adequate to house all of the ranges of man's mind and spirit? In such a case, can both mind and nature, not coinciding or coalescing, neither one enveloping the other, be embraced within the unity of any system which includes them both?

These large, very large questions, are in the background of the subject matter of this chapter. They will there remain for the most part, or be approached but obliquely and with indirection. For before we conclude that mind cannot be domesticated within nature, so that if they are not to remain apart they must be thought of as included within some system which is neither mind nor nature exclusively, we ought to see how far we can go in viewing nature as the home of mind, and what manner of nature it is which can enjoy the tenantry of mind. The question comes to us in this way, rather than the other way around, because from the start we have thought of nature as in any case the habitat of mind and experience. It is nature which stretches out beyond us, and if either is to be integrated within the other it is nature which will include mind, and not mind which will hold nature completely within itself.

We are to consider, then, what it might mean to domesticate mind within nature, thereby ceasing to view mind and experience and consciousness as things apart from the processes, energies, and organized structures which we ascribe to nature. In facing these issues, in seeking what it would mean to integrate mind within nature, so that mind will cease to be something apart from nature, some non-natural or supernatural intruder, two broad, divergent paths have opened out in modern philosophy. The difference between these two divergent directions cannot be stated in terms of any one single issue. Along each of these two paths is to be found a conspectus and synthesis, a comprehensive judgment and assessment of the way in which all the evidence bears upon the issues at stake. One aspect of the

philosophical divergence here in question has to do, to put
it much too simply, with the question as to how much mind
is to be found in nature. Our own minds we know. We know
them because we are minds, living through our experiences. It is plausible to ascribe some mind and experience to
some few other animals. But are we entitled to ascribe to the
whole of nature any more mind than just this recognizable
mind which we come across in familiar places, embodied in
the living bodies of men and of at least some other animals?
On the one hand are those philosophers who, in putting
mind back into nature, do not believe themselves entitled
to increase the amount or range of mind beyond that which
is in evidence in human and animal experience or behavior.
Throughout the vast extent of nature, there is nothing to
indicate that anything resembling mind is discoverable.
Mind there is, sporadic, incidental, appearing when animal
bodies have attained a certain level of organization and certain kinds of interaction with surrounding things.

The second highway is traversed by philosophies which,
in putting mind back into nature, find it necessary to ascribe
to that nature qualities, structures, or relations which themselves depend in some manner upon the presence of mind,
so that nature wears a different aspect in these two different
versions of the amount (to put it crudely) of mind in the
universe. There is also the question as to kinds and degrees
of mind, of structures which approximate to mind, but
which are not fully grown minds.

If mind were itself definable in terms of something we
know to be widely prevalent throughout nature, in terms say
of energy, kinetic or potential, or motion, or organization,
the matter would be fairly simple. There would then be
enough mind to go around, to spread over the whole of
nature. Or if we adopted a theory of panpsychism mind

would be universal, present wherever matter may exist. These are speculative possibilities which carry weight, but they lie a little to one side of the issue with which we are here chiefly concerned. Panpsychism seems to be somewhat too easy a way of putting mind back into nature. And it springs, I think, from a conception of mind in terms of mental phenomena. It is an offshoot of the theory of psycho-physical parallelism, become cosmic and universal. And I would hesitate to put mind into nature through conceiving of mind as itself a form of energy. The utter disparity and incommensurability of conscious experience, of conscious-ness, with physical transactions in space and time, the ulti-macy of consciousness, its essential indefinability, stand in the way of such an identification. It hovers too closely on the edge of reductionism.

The method of integrating mind within nature which will interest us here is somewhat different. It moves in the direction indicated by the following two steps. First, mind and consciousness are viewed not as any unique kind of exist-ent or modality of being, but as a region or dimension, char-acterized by certain types of relation. The central thing about mind is the presence of such relations and relational structures. Secondly, these relations, in terms of which mind is defined, pervade the domain of nature and are ascribed to nature, in her own right. It follows that mind is not set over against nature, contrasted with her life and organization. Mind falls within nature and belongs to her as indefeasibly as do any physical and non-mental structures and events. I need not remind you with what profundity and imagination Woodbridge broke ground along this highway. Now the re-lations in question, those which are definitional of mind, are those which fall within the broad category of meaning. Un-questionably, meanings are to be counted among the posses-

sions of the mind and some account of these meanings will
provide us with our start.

The possessions of the mind are not restricted to only the
immediacies which come and go with the fluctuations of consciousness. Were they so limited, there would be ample justification for looking elsewhere than to mind and consciousness for the organization and stability required for both
man's life and his knowledge. Upon the body would fall the
responsibility for all that man does, all the activities in
which he engages, all his knowing, purposing, and dream-
ing. And were his knowledge limited to his awareness of the
fleeting contents of his immediate possessions, he would be
closed behind doors which shut him off from the world
which he seeks to know. Were his experiences thus restricted,
he could not even imagine that the world to which he was
restricted was a prison.

Besides its immediate experiences, the mind also possesses
meanings. The wisdom of using this term "meaning" which
is in so many ways multivalent may be seriously questioned.
Is there anything other than signs and symbols, or things
functioning as signs and symbols, to which meanings may be
ascribed? It is instructive to observe that we do employ the
verb "to mean" where signs and symbols are absent. I may
be asked what I mean to do. Meaning is here an intention.
And an intention is a tendency, a stretching, an activity
which is proleptic and prospective. It might be suggested,
not too implausibly, that we have here a more primitive
sense of meaning than that which we have when we say that
i means $\sqrt{-1}$. The sense of active tendency, of propulsion
and stretching forward or reaching out, is here the root idea.
As such, it would fall within the perspective of animism, as
that term has here been used. In another sense, meaning ap-
plies not to signs and symbols, nor to intentions, but to

things which, we say, have meaning. When I say "I know now what this means," I may be referring to symbols, for instance, a phrase in a foreign tongue. But I need not do this. I may be referring to the fact that I now see the thing in some context, some set of relations, which enable me now **to understand it** and make sense of it. The context may be of the most various kinds. It may be a casual context, a context of resemblance, the function which the thing has, and so forth. In all these types of meaning, and others which might be mentioned, there is present more than just one item, a single term, with well-defined boundaries. Either there are two terms, spanned by a meaning relation or, as in the case of an intention, a reference to or tendency toward something which lies ahead or beyond. Meaning is never exemplified in a situation containing but a single, self-contained, and bounded entity. Meaning is relational.

Now both man's life and his knowledge would be bankrupt were his experience bounded by his immediate possessions, where each item in experience is some such single term, having no relation to what lies beyond, whether it be some other term or simply that which means, refers to, and tends towards. Some manner of venturing beyond the indubitably given is requisite for both life and knowledge. The possession of what is directly given and present needs to be supplemented by something. Self-evident principles, certified by reason or intuition, common-sense belief, animal faith, the necessities of action blindly relied upon, synthetic principles of organization, are some of the things philosophers have appealed to in order to go beyond the immediacies of the given and the possessed. The question as to the means by which men do pass beyond the frontiers of the immediately given, will be judged to be a specious problem only on the premise that there are no such present immediacies. This is, I suppose, a question of fact, to be settled by the appeal to experience. But what can this mean except the appeal to what someone is experiencing, and is possessing in his actual experience? Nevertheless, the question is misleading and impossible to answer if it be taken to imply that the course of man's experience involves a transition from a stage in which the mind has nothing but its own immediate experience to a later stage in which somehow the mind has miraculously broken through the barriers which formerly had shut it in. For there never was such a stage. Throughout, the mind is in possession of more than its immediately given experiences. Meanings, too, are in its possession, and it is through its meanings that the mind opens out upon a world stretching before it, and it is through its meanings that experiences are organized into the kind of system which makes it possible to speak of a mind and a self. I would place the burden of extricating man from the perplexities of subjectivism and the egocentric dilemma upon the meanings which belong to all the immediacies of his experience throughout.

Experience has a kind of architecture. Experience is individual, and the owner of experience may be thought of as the center of a series of concentric circles or, better, spheres. Or again, the owner is at the focus of a cone spreading out before him. These are geometric analogies, and in the next chapter there will be something to say about the role of analogy and metaphor in thinking about mind and experience. The center or focus is not a point. It has thickness. It is no *focus imaginarius*. An inner circle or sphere nearest the center holds the mind's immediate experiences. Here are the mind's intimate possessions, so intimate that they are constituents of his self, states of his own conscious experience. As one moves outward, there are immediate possessions which are not constituents of the mind. They are immediately experienced, but they fall on the side of things. Such are the apparent shapes of things, the sensible qualities which things present. Now all these immediate possessions are the vehicles and bearers of meanings. Each of them is experienced as incomplete, fragmentary, requiring that it be filled out. It is experienced and possessed as meaning that to which it refers. It is no substitute nor representative of the object which it means. The object is presented directly through the experience which is in our possession because of the meaning of which the experience is the bearer. Through the meanings which the mind has, there are no bounds set to the extent of the world which may be brought within my awareness. But this in no way serves to obliterate the distinction and contrast between that which I possess (immediacies together with their meanings) and the things of which I become aware.

Point may be given to this by recalling how very much more one may be aware of and cognize than that of which he has an actual experience. The adjective "actual" provides the key. Actual experience is what is being enacted and what is present and possessed while it is being enacted. Actual experience is limited to the present, not a durationless instant, but a span, a specious present. I have no actual experience of the past or the future. The past is gone and the future is not yet. Neither can be a present possession. But my awareness is not limited to this ever-moving present. The past is remembered and the future is anticipated. There is that in my actual, immediate, present experience which means the past or the future, and through that meaning with which immediacy is invested, I am aware of past and future. When I am thirsty, I have no actual experience of the quenching of my thirst. Had I such, my thirst would vanish. But I am aware of what will quench my thirst and I desire it. All of which I have an actual experience exists, here and now, in my experience, quite literally. It is enacted. But it is the carrier of a meaning. I am aware in memory of a pain which I experienced last year. It is no part of any thing which I now actually experience, yet I cognize it and am aware of it. Something there is in my present experience, some immediate possession, which is the vehicle through which I have a memory of the past. The present possession has a meaning referring to that past. Hume's impressions are possessions of actual experience. Disregard the question as to whether, for Hume, they are mental, non-mental, or neutral entities. In any case they are possessed in immediate experience. Hume is zealous to insist that this is all that they are. An impression holds no meaning which refers beyond its own boundaries. Now ideas are, for Hume, faint revivals and copies of impressions. Their whole being is exhausted in the fact of their presence, in being possessed. Yet Hume constantly treats these ideas as if they were ideas of the impressions which they resemble; as if the fact of resemblance and derivation entitled the idea to an awareness of its ancestry. In any idea which is an idea of its original, both immediacy and objective reference, both possession and meaning, are present.

Again, there is no actual experience of possibilities, for possibilities are not as yet enacted and they may never be; no possibility can be the content of an actual experience. But possibilities enter my awareness in countless ways. I discover them. They are not fictions. They enter into the structure of things as I am aware of them and all of my practical and purposive activities depend upon the awareness of possibilities. Moreover, the recognition of conscious life other than my own comes within this general framework. I have no

actual experience of the experiences which have their focus
in other minds. Yet I am surely aware of them, and I acknowledge them. This awareness is not of the same order as
an inductive inference. It is more direct and compelling. It
is analogous to the awareness of past and future, which itself
is not an inference from present data. These examples are
cited merely as illustrations of the vast discrepancy between
actually experiencing, and being cognizant of. What lies beyond immediacy is apprehended through the meanings with
which our actual possessions are invested and of which they
are the bearers and vehicles.

It is this interplay of possession and meaning which makes
it possible to project experience upon a scale with two ideal
limits, a lower limit of sentiency, sheer possession, lacking
all meaning, and an upper limit of bare meanings and
essences conveying no hint of possession, of actuality. These
are ideal limits, definable in thought, but not descriptive of
any experience which we know. Whether the experience of
an amoeba consists entirely in the presence of momentary
flashes of sentiency, conveying no meaning, containing no
hint of more to come, no reference to what impends ahead
and beyond, can only be guessed. The presumption is
against any such supposition. To endow any creature with
such a meaningless possession is not in keeping with what we
know of nature's strategy. Such bare sentiency is the ideal
limit of a projection backwards in which meaning dimin-
ishes to the vanishing point. The ideal upper limit is a projection in the opposite direction. It gives us a realm of meanings and essences completely severed from the actuality of
experienced possessions. It is an extrapolation of the tension
between possession and meaning as actual experience di-
minishes to the vanishing point, leaving meanings to float
off, unhinged from any connection with actuality. Short of

and between these two ideal limits, our experience lives and moves.

The large areas of man's experience which are marked off as aesthetic, practical, and theoretical, are definable, in part at least, in terms of the different relations between possession and meaning characteristic of each of them. It is characteristic of man's experience as aesthetic that there should be a fusion, ideally a complete fusion, of what is actually possessed in experience and its meaning. What is present and given does not lead off and point to something distant. The meaning conveyed by what is present and experienced is embodied and incorporated in the experience which is possessed. The qualities and rhythms of sound and color, had and immediately possessed, are experienced as themselves the adequate embodiment of significant meanings. The aesthetic experience is the possession of an object which is what it ought to be. There are no hints of meanings pointing beyond, not as yet embodied in the mind's possessions. The field of awareness coincides with the actual experience the content of which is sufficiently rich to be fully satisfying. Nor is there any superfluous overplus of meaningless data and possessions. What is had is completely satisfying. Aesthetic experience may seem to be a fruition too good to be true. It is, as it were, a foretaste of heaven. It is the stilling and consummation of restless striving, of all the insecurity and dissatisfaction bred by both the failure of our possessions to disclose any meaning, and the awareness of meanings for which no embodiment and vehicle can be found amongst any of our actual possessions. It has not seldom been taken to belong not to the main currents of experience, but to sheltered areas remote from the serious business of living. The aesthetic object is framed and insulated in order to bar the possible intrusion of irrelevant meanings and extraneous data.

The tension between art and morality is an ancient theme, from Plato to Tolstoy and William James. The aesthetic segment of experience appears anomalous when measured in terms of man's experience as striving, as purposive, and also as cognitive. For neither in man's experience as practical, or moral, or theoretic, is there any such coalescence of possession and meaning as characterizes aesthetic experience. What is given and had is incomplete and inadequate. We want something which we do not have, and we have something which we do not understand, because it is divorced from the meaning which it should have, if it were to become meaningful and intelligible. There is an aspect of ideality, of tension, between what we actually possess and the meaning which would be required to complete it, in all these sectors of man's experience which are contrasted with his experience as aesthetic. Man's experience is not restricted to the immediacies which are his actual and present possessions. The mind also is in possession of meanings which penetrate all of experience, and whose presence generates the features which are most characteristic of man's living and experiencing.

The point of all this, for our present discussion, lies in the fact that meaning is a category which is derived solely from experience, that is to say, from *mind*. We become acquainted with meanings, we know what meanings mean, because of what transpires in our experience. Meaning is a category fetched from the perspective of animism. Not all of the categories in terms of which we do our thinking are derived from the perspective of animism. There are those which come from the observer's perspective. Space and coexistence in space, time as the sequence of happenings, observed relations among events, correlations and functional variations, categories such as these come not from the perspective of animism but from the observer's perspective. Time, within the animistic perspective, is not the same as time in the observer's perspective. In dealing with all such categories, the question as to where they have been derived from, where, so to speak, their native and original home is to be found, is of the first importance.

The initial and inescapable contrast between the two perspectives, between experience and nature, leads us to expect that the categories derived from either one of these will differ markedly from those categories which are derived from the other. The original home of the category of meaning in all its different forms is experience. The meanings found there are mind-dependent. It is in our experience that we learn what meanings mean, just as it is within the perspective of animism that we learn what it is to exist as a mind and self, or what it means to have the immediacies of actual experience. We have to resort to experience as lived within the perspective of animism to come upon the meanings with which our actual and immediate experiences are invested. Our question now becomes, How far are we warranted in taking the meanings which belong to experience and ascribing them to nature, describing her structures and processes in terms of categories derived from experience? To do this carries the implication that mind is also there where nature is. Nature, so interpreted and described, is no longer closed to mind.

Thus far, nothing has been said about consciousness and our question assumes a somewhat different shape when we introduce that aspect or quality of experience which the adjective "conscious" denotes. To what extent and in what manner is consciousness requisite for the presence and deployment of meanings? Consciousness so far has appeared to be the seat of immediacy, signifying the presence in actual experience of that which is most intimately and immediately in the mind's possession. Consciousness is also, we have seen, that without which nothing would matter, in any sense in which things that matter make a difference in terms of the better and the worse, in terms of value. Values are dependent on consciousness. Are meanings likewise dependent on consciousness, coming into being only within the matrix and dimension supplied by consciousness? The role played by consciousness, as well as the relation between consciousness and meaning, may be approached through a consideration of certain fundamental forms of meaning, the analysis of which is nowhere carried through with greater insight than in James's famous chapter "The Stream of Thought" in his *Psychology*. The meanings here analyzed are those which are present in what is actually being experienced. All of them are concerned with the way in which the "passing thought," the immediately felt content, means that which itself is not, and thereby is the bearer of a meaning which points beyond, and which tends, stretches, and means that which lies beyond itself. Here are anticipatory, prevenient meanings, pointing to that which lies ahead. And there are purposive meanings, active tendencies, moving in the direction of their own fulfillment.

James's exposition gives powerful support to the view that all these meanings require consciousness as the medium in which to exist and come to life, just as a fish needs water in which to live. This is what we would expect if the category of meaning is originally derived from the perspective of animism. James's chapter moves entirely within that perspective. Consummatory and anticipatory meanings are carried by every momentary pulse within the stream of thought, within conscious experience. Each passing moment is suffused with a sense of what has gone before and

what is about to come. It is experienced as loaded with
these meanings. There is more to the present experience
than just a present event which has replaced a previous
event and which will in turn be replaced by its successor.
Memory and anticipation are here because there is a mind
which is more than successiveness, a mind which appropri-
ates and possesses its own successive vicissitudes, in a manner which has no analogy with anything discernible in nature where there is no mind, or with anything encompassed
within the observer's perspective.

Recall the account of the feeling of thunder, which is also
a feeling of the silence as just gone. The thunder, as actually
heard, is suffused with a quality derived from the silence
which has gone. But the silence, as a state of physical nature,
has completely gone and vanished when comes the thunder.
The thunder supersedes and replaces the silence. But in our
conscious experience the silence has not been completely
superseded. It lingers on, endowing the thunder as heard
with a meaning which the thunder as a physical event cannot possibly have. Had James been writing a chapter in
meteorology, describing the sequence of nature's events
during a thunderstorm, rather than a chapter on the stream
of thought, on the course of man's experience of the storm,
he never would have reported the persistence of silence
after it had been displaced by thunder. Thunder, as a physical event, is what it is and nothing else. It contains no inkling of the silence that went before. The silence has entirely
vanished. The experience of thunder, as an event in the
"concrete consciousness of man" (the phrase is James's) is a
possession of experience which has a meaning, lacking in
the physical occurrence.

What is possessed in conscious experience also has meanings which point ahead and are anticipatory of the future.

Expectancy and premonition are there, feelings of the direction in which events are moving, a reference to what is not as yet in our possession. There is a sense of the direction from which an impression is about to come, although no positive impression is yet there. What is present and possessed is felt as incomplete, as requiring, for the development of its own meaning, something further which at the moment lies ahead and is not yet in our possession. Thus, a musical cadence which does not terminate in a tonic chord is—or used to be—felt as incomplete and hanging in the air. It means something which it has not achieved. As a physical event, as a set of vibrations or just as a sound in nature, it is no more incomplete than is the final chord of a classical sonata. It has all manner of antecedent and consequent events, but it is indifferent to them. It might be preceded or followed by any sound whatever. It is only in man's conscious experience, only in what James depicts as the stream of thought, that things and events have anticipatory and consummatory meanings.

There is an added increment of meaning when there is not only an anticipatory awareness of what is to come, but when, as in conation and striving, there is the active tendency to achieve something lying as yet in the future. The concept of active tendency is animistic. Its home is in the perspective of animism. It has its source in no observed concatenation of events related solely in terms of temporal sequence and spatial conjunctions. It is derived from experience, from what we live through and experience in our own strivings and doings. The history of science exhibits the progressive elimination of agencies, of forces, of active tendencies, of causes which make things happen and which generate their effects. These are occult qualities not revealed in the observable sequence of nature's events.

They have no legitimate place in the descriptive formulation of the regularities of space-time events. The phenomenal manifold, as it appears within the observer's perspective, offers items to be correlated, and the formulation of such functional relations is the chief business of the scientific observer of things. Are the processes of nature, the birth of suns and galactic systems, the episodes which comprise the history of planets, the aggregation of elements to form rocks and rivers, soil and atmosphere, and the living bodies of plants and animals, do these titanic histories disclose active tendencies, striving for the attainment of any ends? We allocate a privileged status to certain occurrences and call them beginnings and endings. We thus dramatize the transactions of nature, envisage the entrance of new actors and agents, let them run their course and disappear. An act has been enacted. Were the natural sciences to complete their story of all these happenings, how many of these dramatic beginnings and endings would be dissolved into the restless continuum of events, or the persistence throughout of energies and entities which remain wholly constant, untroubled by the comings and goings of any individual actors? I do not know the answer to this question. We are entitled to say, with some safety, that whatever novel qualities may present themselves and mark the beginning of something new, these beginnings and endings are viewed either as rearrangements and fresh collocations of the elements comprising them, or they are correlated with other happenings and qualities in terms of space-time coordinates. The further the analysis can be pushed, the greater will be the degree of regularity, uniformity, and predictability in the sequence of observed and observable events. A functional equation, descriptive of verifiable correlations of events, change here correlated with change there, permitting an equation or graph of the manner in which a dependent variable changes with its argument—this is the objective of all scientific observation, experiment, and hypothesis. A differential equation is the ideal of every science.

In meteorology and seismology, in biology, psychology, and economics, the analysis of gross events into their more ultimate constituents has not been carried as far as in physics. We have not yet learned to predict or to control earthquakes, the incidence of cancer, or of poverty. But these sciences are still young. Within the framework of the observed, inferred, and described, within the nature with which the sciences deal, there is no place for meanings, whether consummatory, anticipatory, or purposive. There are no active tendencies. There are relations, correlations of space-time variables. Hume's account of causality is an authentic transcript of the working procedures of the sciences, and what they report. Y varies with X, is correlated with X, accompanies X in space or follows it in time. This is the language here appropriate. When we translate this into the language of meaning and say that Y means X, or X means Y, we have to be on our guard. If the statement that smoke means fire is intended only to report the fact that smoke and fire are correlated, spatially and temporarily, well and good. If we say that smoke means fire, in the sense of being a sign of fire, we are reporting something in addition to such a correlation. We are drawing upon our experience, our consciousness, in which smoke is in our possession, is experienced; and this possession has a meaning. It is only in the medium of conscious experience, where belong such intentions, leadings, anticipations and memories; it is only in the perspective of animism that something can have meaning. In nature, events just follow one another. Mead writes that "metaphysically things are their meanings. The world is ceaselessly becoming what it means." In saying this, he is saved by his use of the adverb "metaphysically." Scientifically things have antecedents and consequences. They do not mean them, save as these things are given an ontological status analogous to that of the passing thought in James's chapter. We observe no anticipation, expectancy, or any reference to the past in any observed event. The lowering sky has no premonition of the coming storm, and when the storm has run its course—how anthropomorphic is this language!—it is followed by uprooted trees, blocked mountain passes, and overflowing rivers. In this sequence of events there is no hazard, no uncertainty, no success or failure, no expectancy, none of the meanings which are the categories derived from conscious experience, from the "stream of thought" and from the perspective of animism. The time in which nature's events transpire is not the same time as that in which experience is lived. The mind holds together in its experience events which, when viewed within the observer's perspective, are not held together, but follow upon one another. The occurrence of an event supersedes preceding events, to be in turn superseded by following events, one thing after another, each replacing its predecessor, is nature's version of time. The version yielded by experience is different. Conscious events are grouped and organized in a fashion which no mere succession of events could possibly exemplify.

All of this might be admitted so far as inanimate nature, the motions of planets, the erosion of soil, and the course of storms are concerned. But in observing living animals and the behavior of their bodies, do we not discern meanings, over and above the sequences and correlations of phenomena? Do we not see the anticipatory, expectant attitude of the cat, poised to spring on a mouse, the dog waiting for his dinner? Surely, here is more than the sequence and correlation of observed events. Two brief comments have here to be made. First, we either do or do not impute to the cat some measure and level of conscious experience, some degree and kind of mind, totally unlike anything which we ascribe to the cloud, save when we are animistic and not scientific. If we do endow the cat with conscious experience, then the cat's present posture and behavior can legitimately be described in terms of its reference to the future. It has a prevenient meaning. If we do not endow the cat with conscious experience, then we have no more basis for ascribing expectancy to its present attitude than we have to say that a boulder poised on the edge of a precipice, is expectant of the motions in space which will probably ensue. My second comment is this. Even if we do suppose ourselves justified in ascribing experience to the cat, for the purpose of scientific observation, prediction, and control, all that will interest us is a formulation of the probable consequences of the present state of affairs, with respect to the situation containing the cat and the mouse. All behavioristic psychology is there to prove it. At most, such terms as "expectancy" and "anticipation" are convenient shorthand devices, telescoping what, if expanded, becomes the formulation of a generalized law of antecedents and consequences. If they are more than this, if they denote meanings which pertain to the dimension of conscious experience, then they are more and other than observed phenomena in space-time.

When I read, as I sometimes do, that the processes and events of "nature" are perplexing, obscure, fragmentary, uncertain, problematic, and precarious, that "nature" ex-

hibits creative advance, that there are anticipatory premonitions of things to come, and active tendencies striving
to make them come, I know that I am hearing about a
nature described in categories fetched from man's conscious experience. Whitehead's philosophy provides a striking instance of offering an interpretation of nature in
terms drawn from the domain of conscious experience.
Whitehead does, I think, play fast and loose with the notion of consciousness. It is, on the one hand, flickering and
evanescent. "It is the crown of experience, only occasionally
attained, not its necessary base." [1] On the other hand, every
actual occasion throughout the entire world of nature
possesses sentiency. It is a sentient experience. It holds
memory of the past, immediacy of realization, in the enacted present and indication of things to come. Only actual
occasions exist, and each actual occasion is "the self-
enjoyment of importance." [2] But this sentiency, physical
and "propositional feelings," subjective aims and values,
are uncontaminated with the quality of consciousness. Nature, envisaged in Whiteheadean terms, is living on borrowed capital. The debt is acknowledged by Whitehead,
if not by nature. "In this sketch, upon analysis, more concrete than that of the scientific scheme of thought, I have
started from our own psychological field." [3] He has picked
up the meanings which James discovered in the stream
of thought, and he describes nature in terms of these meanings, minimizing, if not deleting, the only medium in which
these meanings can have any status, that of consciousness
and mind.

His philosophy, in this respect, is an instance of the

1 Alfred North Whitehead, *Process and Reality* (New York, 1929), p. 408.
2 *Modes of Thought* (New York, 1938), p. 150.
3 *Science and the Modern World* (New York, 1925), p. 107.

desire to have all the benefits derivable from the use of the term "experience," without any of the responsibilities which would be entailed by the recognition of consciousness. Both spirit and nature are embraced within the generous folds of experience, with the result, I think, that scant justice is done to the distinctive features and the integrity of either. Is there any conclusion to which such considerations as those which have been offered may appear to point? It is the bifurcation and duality which is problematic, shutting man's mind out of nature, and estranging man's conscious life from the energies and structures which belong to nature. Of course, if nature were defined as the totality of all existence, then it would be obvious that man and all the possessions of his mind belong to nature. But within *this* nature, all the old contrasts and dualities would break out afresh, and we would need a new name to denote that which man sets over against his own life.

A poor and improverished nature, stripped down to such a skeleton as was pictured by the older mechanistic and materialistic theories, cannot accommodate the wealth of meanings which man possesses in his own life and experience. And so we set about to add to nature's contents, and to the existence which is hers by right. We restore to her the qualities of sound and color, taste and smell. We let her have life, for all living forms have sprung from her, sustained by what she can give them, and by the give and take between living organisms and the habitat which surrounds them. We give nature organization. Everywhere, nature is replete with structure, system, and organization. We describe her minutest parts in terms of complexly organized fields and systems of mutual interdependencies. And finally we give her meanings and meaningful relations. There is life and movement, creative advance and novelty, and each surge of nature's processes is both a cumulative propension, inheriting the content of what has gone before and providing a thrust forward, presaging and giving promise of what is to come. Thus to read nature in terms of meanings is to view her as the scene of a drama, never ending, but one in which there are beginnings and endings. Within such acts, there is meaningful development, the unfolding of a theme, even if the drama as a whole has no single theme. All these meanings in terms of which the life and organization, the structures and processes within nature are depicted, imply that there is more in nature than coexistences in space and sequences and supersessions in time. Nature is characterized by relational structures and systems which are additional to, and which supervene upon, the framework of space and time. Space and time relations are there, but only as a matrix within which new and different types of order are exhibited and developed. And all of these supervening relations and structures are meaningful relations and meaningful structures. Here are individual entities, individual continuants, each one exemplifying the prevenience of some one dominant theme which requires just this sequence of events and just this type of organization for its realization. Nature takes on not only such meanings as these, but in doing so, she becomes the scene in which values are achieved. For the notion of value is there in the offing, when we speak of meaning. Meaninglessness is absence of all worth and significance. So nature can now house value and beauty, harmony and charm, as well as meaning. There is purpose there, fruition, and achievement, together with frustration and defeat. There are active tendencies, leadings, and strivings. And all of these significant relations which are now native within nature, are types and variants of meaning and meaningful relations. How like the human world has nature become! The gap which had erstwhile divided man from nature has been filled. Man finds in his own life and history, in the meanings which his own experience possesses, just what he might expect to find, being, as he is, a child of nature. These meanings lent to man's life by nature, for a brief span, become invested with greater freedom, they become more concentrated, and they generate, in man, potentialities of control and expansion which nature nowhere else exhibits. They make possible the life of intelligence and reason. But they are all of the same stuff as is found in nature, for nature is the home of meanings. We have learned to put into nature that which an older science and philosophy denied her, and all of man's mind and spirit is domesticated within nature.

But notice. All these meanings are variants, and further developments of anticipatory, consummatory, and purposive meanings. And the original home of these meanings is in man's conscious experience, in the "stream of thought." It is here that these meanings are first found. They exist here, in the medium of mind and of consciousness. Without this matrix of conscious life, there would be no such meanings, no premonitions, no cumulative continuation of what has gone before, no active tendencies pressing toward their own fruition. Without this dimension and matrix, supplied by mind and conscious experience, there would be a succession of happenings, each superseding and pushing out its predecessor. There would be before and after, supersession and succession, but no living present which itself holds the past and the future together without letting the one slip away, and the other be just nothing. There would be one thing after another, and that is all.

The question which would seem to press is whether we

can take all these relations of meaning, describe nature in terms dependent upon such meaningful contexts, without acknowledging the debt which is owed to the dimension of being from whence all these meaning relations have been derived. If we are right in conceiving nature in these terms, if nature does contain this wealth of meaning, how are we to suppose that these meanings can now live and thrive when drawn off from the only context and dimension in which we know them to exist? For we know them, in the first instance, as meanings which are the mind's possessions. They belong to the perspective of animism. If nature is more or other than that which comes within the observer's perspective, we now have an animism which goes beyond the perspective of animism with which so far we have been concerned. Within that perspective, man's mind and experience is set over against a world in which none of the characteristics of mind, its immediate experiences or its meanings, are in evidence. Now in this expanded and enriched nature, man discovers meanings which, within the narrower perspective of animism, he had supposed belonged only to him.

It has been written that "as such, nature is itself wistful and pathetic, turbulent and passionate. Were it not, the existence of wants would be a miracle." Where, one asks, do wistfulness and pathos, turbulence and passion, reside? Do any of the authentic sciences, dispassionately observing the sequence of events anywhere, come upon these traits?

I have asked questions without answering them. They belong to those unformulated problems which provide the background for what has been under consideration in this chapter.

We are in the end confronted with two alternatives. We may take the insight supplied by the observer's perspective, by the sciences, as yielding the only authentic knowledge of nature which is accessible to us. That nature will be compacted of events, structures, and relations, all of which, in the last analysis and ideally, are statable in terms of space-time continuities and relations. In this nature there are no meanings and no values. Things just are, and events just happen. The mind, with all of its possessions, its immediacies and its meanings would appear to be a miracle in such a world, a miracle such as human wants would be, were not nature wistful and passionate. It would cease being a miracle, on these premises, only if we ignored and failed to note the experiences through which man lives, the immediacies which are the possessions of his conscious life. It would cease to be a miracle if consciousness were identified with the behavior of animal bodies and the functions which they perfom. What stands in the way of this is just that which is yielded by the perspective of animism, and it is this which one has to reckon.

Or we may think of a nature domiciled with significant structures and meaningful relations, a nature which does not quite coincide with that nature presented by the sciences within the observer's perspective. It is a nature which wears some of the aspects of mind. Along the path of the first alternative, mind is something of an anomaly. In the second alternative, nature becomes something of an anomaly. She becomes much more mysterious than she had ever been before. She becomes a nature which, as it were, seeks man out, creating his mind so that he too can enjoy the wealth of meanings that is hers. It is as if nature were not content just to be and to happen, to enact her own drama unseen and unwitnessed. She wants a spectator, and she brings forth mind in order that the drama shall not go on without an audience, without a mind to witness and enjoy, and to participate in the life that is hers, and in order that nature may herself become the instrument and servant of the child she has brought forth. This is a metaphor and, perchance, myth and symbol. How far man's mind, in searching to wrest from nature and from his own life the secrets they contain, may penetrate without the use of metaphor and symbol, this question will send us on to our next and last chapter.

CHAPTER V

The Mind's Excursive Power

LANGUAGE IS STEEPED IN METAPHOR. THE title of this chapter is a metaphor; the mind goes on no excursion in physical space. We readily accord to the poet the privilege of inventing metaphors, playing with them, and allowing the images which they evoke to hover before the mind. The more sober and pedestrian use of language should, we suppose, free itself from metaphor. We would like our science and our philosophy to employ language which is anchored to matter of fact, to be a transcript of things as they are, to be literal and not metaphorical. The structures built up in human discourse, if they are to convey knowledge, should duplicate the structures exemplified in things known. They should, like a good photograph, be faithful to their originals. But notice, I have just employed a metaphor. The mind, or the discourse which it utters and formulates, is a photographic plate or a wax tablet, waiting to receive the impress to be made upon it. And how many are the metaphors which men have used in their language about man's mind! It is a searchlight which illumines that on which its rays fall. Have not I fallen back on metaphor in speaking of the mind as a spectator, as if knowing were like an act of vision? Metaphors creep in when men give other versions of what it means to know. Knowing is a practical art. The knower refashions and reconstructs things, making them more suitable for man's life, as a builder might reconstruct a house, or a painter touch up a picture. Indeed, if one is to say what anything is, must he not say that it is something which it resembles, or else fall back on the tautology that it is what it is? Resemblances are the seeds of metaphor.

The fact that language is so full of metaphor, together with the fact that men's thinking is so dependent upon linguistic symbols, strongly suggests that the ways of language are not the ways of things, that there is some hiatus here, some rift between both thought and discourse on the one hand and the nature of things on the other. When things enter the mind (a metaphor derived from space) they expand, proliferate, and grow, as do bacteria when immersed in a proper culture. The longer they remain in the mind, the greater is their divergence from the shapes which they had before they left the world whence they have wandered into the mind. If the mind could only halt them just as they crossed its threshold and hold them fast, it might hope to capture things unamended and unspoiled. This very propensity, woven into all discourse, to speak in metaphor and parable would appear to mark the wide disparity between discourse and things. There are no metaphors or parables in nature.

The rift between discourse and the things which discourse would be about, between what Santayana has called "concretions in existence" and "concretions in discourse," has grown apace as men have reflected upon the nature of the symbols which they employ. As these symbols have become refined and perfected in symbolic logic and pure mathematics they have less and less to tell us about existence. The symbols are all defined, with the exception, perhaps, of some few initial indefinables, and we know just what to do with these. Their manipulation is a game of substitution. There is no mathematical symbol for which a perfect substitute cannot be found. Equations express such possibilities of substitution. No risk is taken and there is no occasion for any metaphor. If, perchance, some one of the whole numbers were lost and could not be found, say the number six, it would make no real difference. An infinite number of substitutes for six are available. Half of twelve, twice three, the sum of five and one, and so on endlessly—they are all identical, and any one is as good as any other. Here is the perfect model of literalness, purchased at the price of yielding any claim to conveying a knowledge of things. The truths so formulated are trifling and not instructive. The view has been held, by Meyerson for instance, that the search for identities such as these has been one of the main driving forces in man's intellectual life. The mind cannot rest until it has carried through to completion the activity of identification. This is the supreme ideal of theoretic intelligibility, an ideal doomed to perpetual frustration because in existence there are no identities. There are unique qualities, events, and individuals. The procedure of Meyerson is, I think, somewhat Procrustean, in forcing all ideals of what the mind would like to uncover into the single pattern of identification. This ideal is completely realized, in any case, in the realm of mathematical symbols; and this but serves to reinforce our sense of the rift and disparity between symbols and things.

Among the mind's possessions, I have said, are its meanings. How metaphorical is this statement! The mind is an owner. The mind acquires title to things which come into its possession. Who or what held title to them before they became the property of the mind? Does the original owner give up his title, or is there joint ownership? Are things

leased to the mind so that its ownership is conditional? Does
the title revert when the mind relinquishes its ownership?
These are the questions, debated back and forth by idealists and realists, critical realists and new realists. Are these
questions engendered by the metaphor of ownership from
which we start? If we began with another metaphor these
questions would not be asked. There would be a different
set of questions. Try another metaphor then. Say that knowing is a practical art, akin to making or building. At once a
different set of questions confronts us. What is the material
with which the technician or artist works? Why does he
want to make it into something different from what it is?
What are the tools and instruments with which he works,
and how were they fashioned? Whether any question is significant depends on the context within which it is asked,
and in these questions about what the mind is and does the
context depends on the chosen metaphor which is the
springboard from which one leaps. There are many spring-
boards.

The statement that the mind has its meanings, and, presumably, is to do something with its possessions, would be
uttered otherwise by those who believe in the power of symbols but who are hesitant in ascribing to the mind or to consciousness the role of generating or using symbols. It is as if
symbols somehow operated themselves, their operation
being similar to a vast mechanical system of traffic lights
which go on and off automatically. Some such view is remi-
niscent of Hobbes, or of those who, like James, suggest that
it would be more appropriate to use the impersonal form,
"it thinks," than the form "I or my mind is thinking." Flu-
ent writing and speaking does exhibit a high degree of
apparent automatism. But of course no one supposes that
symbols, concretions in discourse, literally manipulate

themselves. There is a mechanism behind these changes and interchanges among symbols. The intricate mechanism of a counting machine, or the still more intricate mechanism of the muscles of the mathematician's fingers, are what achieve the actual manipulations and substitutions. The human body has a marvelous repertoire of sign- and symbol-making mechanisms. Gestures of hand and face, the making of cries and sounds, the cutting of notches in sticks, the drawing of pictograms, making the letters of the alphabet, weaving them into words and sentences—here is the factory which has made and ever makes and remakes the symbols which are used in discourse. If the body can thus fabricate all the symbols used in discourse, can arrange and rearrange them, has not the body achieved its final triumph? It has created the medium in which discourse and thought live. There seems to be little or nothing left which would stand in need of the mind, as anything distinct from the body's making and using of symbols.

The problem of the relation between mind and body, if taken to be a genuine one not fastened upon us by symbols which the body employs, has generally been regarded in terms of the mind's actual and immediate possessions. The felt immediacies of consciousness—pleasures and pain, sensation and feelings—where are they lodged in the brain; or if not there encased, with what brain processes are they correlated, or how do they interact with the currents of nervous energy within the brain? It will be instructive, I think, to shift somewhat the form of the question about the relation of mind and body, and I would ask that we consider the mind's meanings rather than the mind's immediate possessions. What is it that the mind does with its meanings? This, too, is metaphor, as if the mind were a merchant, doing something with his goods, or a collector of stamps doing something to his collection. I would ask whether the mind does something with its meanings which the body cannot do with the things with which it deals, not even with the symbols, sounds and marks, which it contrives. And I would wish that whatever we may learn from this might suggest something about the mind's relation to nature, that nature which I have thus far so zealously tried to keep separate from the mind of man. We shall move very much in the realm of metaphor, as has language itself in all of its concern with the mind.

And first we should frame some notion of the kind of thing that the body does and can do. Not the finer and more ultimate things that the body does, in effecting chemical changes which maintain so marvelously the body temperature, the oxygen needed by the lungs, and the thousand other adjustments which sustain the equilibrium needed for the body's life and growth. It is the gross behavior of the body, taken as a whole, with all of its organs and energies concentrated upon some macroscopic activity, like chopping wood, or playing the piano, or like talking and singing. There is one large and inclusive group of activities which the body performs, in which the hands play a decisive role and give their name to the activities of manipulation. The word has outgrown its exclusive application to things done with the hands, so that we may speak of the cow's manipulation of her cud, or of manipulating the pedals of a car with the feet. Yet the hands deserve to have these activities named after them, because their importance in the development of man and of all his practical arts has been so decisive.

Now what is it that the body does whenever it manipulates anything? The answer is, in principle, quite clear. It takes things apart, pries them loose from where they are found by him, rearranges the parts by moving some of them to other places, and carries things from one place to another; and this is all that it does. From making a flint hatchet to making a canoe or making alloys, digging coal, planting and sowing seed, man is forever manipulating things. He moves or carries things from one place to another. If it is his own body that he thus manipulates, we say that he is walking or running. All of these manipulations occur in the dimensions of space and time, because his body lives within space and time.

The Greek verb to carry is φέρω, and the Latin cognate is likewise *fero*. The same Greek preposition, μετά which interested us in speaking of metaphysics, when prefixed to φέρω, yields "metaphor." A metaphor is a carrying beyond or across. The Latin preposition *trans,* affixed to *fero,* yields "transfer," or "translate," if the participial form of the Latin verb is chosen. "Transfer," "translate," "metaphor," all signify, originally and literally, carrying something over, which is just what the body does whenever it manipulates things. It would surprise us if the company to whom we entrust the manipulation of our luggage were known as, say, the New York Metaphor Company rather than the New York Transfer Company. The practical, manipulating Romans have had their word for "carrying over" selected, rather than the more speculative-minded Greeks. We go to the Greek for a different kind of carrying over and transferring, and we call it metaphor. Here is a primal metaphor, embedded in metaphor itself. For what are carried over in metaphor are not chunks of matter, physical things, dislodged from some place and transferred to another. What the mind carries across in its metaphors are its meanings. And here, I think, is a transferring agency beyond the powers of the body. The very word "manipulate," which has so many rightful uses when applied to what the body does, is out of place when applied to the meanings with which the mind is concerned. One ought not to manipulate or rig up meanings to suit one's convenience.

And so, I would suggest, this is one thing that the mind does with its meanings. It metaphors them from one—can I say place?—to another. But the dimensions in which meanings are transferred can hardly be that of space. That is the body's domain, to be left free for its carryings-over and manipulations. To think of the domain where meanings are ferried and metaphored from one place to another is, of course, once more a metaphor. It is to think of this domain as a dimension, a kingdom or a realm, analogous perhaps to physical space or to a sovereign state. We have no other name but that of mind to designate this dimension, this realm. The realm of mind has now somewhat outgrown the way in which we have so far been viewing it. We have been thinking of mind as an owner, in possession of its immediate experiences and also of its meanings. Now, taking our cue from the body's manipulating of things, transporting them from place to place, we are to look at mind as the dimension in which meanings are carried on, translated, and metaphored. Not the hoarding of its possessions, but the life and activity of doing things with its possessions, especially its meanings, comes now into focus.

I want to see what we can make of this metaphor derived from the body's manipulation of things. I think it may carry us far, remembering all the while that we are not only the makers of metaphor, but the creatures of metaphor as well. I want to suggest some of the ways in which the mind exercises its excursive powers, through the things which happen to its meanings, through what the mind does with its meanings. Mind is not only the habitat of meanings; it is the user

of meanings. We shall need to remember these other possessions of the mind, its actual experiences, the immediacies
of its conscious life; but for the moment we shall think of
the mind in terms of meanings rather than of consciousness.

Jonathan Swift's Academy of Projectors in Lagado, it
will be recalled, had a scheme for abolishing language and
making physical things take the place of words. "Since
words are only names for things, it would be more convenient for all men to carry about with them such physical
things as were necessary to express a particular business
they are to discourse on." They went about, you will recall,
with heavy sacks laden with a great variety of things some
of which they would spread on the floor and point to; then
they would pack them up and go on their next business.
These literal-minded folk are the progenitors of those who
ask that we never talk of anything unless it can be pointed
to, as if all the furniture of the mind could be carried in a
sack and emptied on the table. Semantics is, at times, an
atavistic reversion to the procedure of Swift's projectors in
Lagado.

However, Swift's projectors found it awkward to carry
around a sufficient supply of physical things to meet their
needs, and they had eventually to resort to language. What
is it that language does that physical things cannot do? But
this way of putting the question needs revision. For language does not always operate itself. The psittacisms of a
parrot are not a fair sample of human discourse. We should
put the question thus: What does the mind do with words
which the body cannot do with things? But there is yet another question which needs to be asked first. What can the
mind do with things that the body cannot do? The body
can move, transfer, and, in the literal sense, translate things.
The mind picks out something; it does not manipulate it,

nor transfer it to another place, but it converts it into a sign, a sign of some other thing. Wherever there are signs and symbols some mind has been at work, just as some body has been working when we see the things of physical nature reshaped into tractors and houses. In space and time, where things exist and events happen, there are no signs. There are antecedents, consequences, and coincidences. There is plenty of manipulation in physical nature, extending the range of this term beyond the manipulations effected by animal bodies. This is the physical nature, of course, which houses and incorporates no mind. When the mind makes a thing into a sign, a meaning is born; and the thing is invested with a meaning which it did not have as an item in nature's sequence of events. But this is just the beginning. For the mind is going to do something to these meanings which it has created. It is going to carry them over, metaphor them, from one content to another. To do this, the mind has to pry the meaning loose from its first habitat or embodiment, in order to carry it over to some other content. Now language is the prime instrument whereby meanings are detached from their original locus and translated to some other occasion or situation. This is to say in different language what has already been said about the mind's possessions. Things, possessed and had in actual experience, come to us, are given to us, with meanings. They mean more than they are. They come to us as a kind of natural sign, giving to man a hint that he can make signs, and do on a larger scale what is achieved in the fusion and interplay of immediate data and meanings in his own conscious life. Something akin to this power to see things as signs, if not to make them into signs, antedates human life. Wherever it is found, there is evidence of the existence of mind. A man-like ape sees a crooked stick as something which he can use to bring a banana within reach. The stick means more than what it is immediately sensed as being. But the meaning is tied down to the concrete, particular circumstances which convey or embody that meaning. The meaning has not yet become explicit and articulate. Not yet has it been pried loose. There is no linguistic symbol to convey the meaning as such. The stick is a sign of what it can be used for. But, as James puts it, this sign is drowned in its own direct import. It cannot be lifted out and metaphored or translated elsewhere.

Sherrington propounds a more than rhetorical question in asking, "When a dog stops tiptoe with lifted head awaiting the strange dog, are we to suppose he has no general notion of 'strange dog'?" If, indeed, the notion is there as a meaning which the dog apprehends, it is there but implicitly, woven and tied into the perception of the strange individual dog now confronting him. Language is required for meanings to become explicit, detached, and transferable. The mind does with these meanings something analogous to what the body does with its manipulanda. I can pluck the rose from the bush, but not in this manipulating way can I pluck the bloom from the rose, nor the grin from any but the Cheshire cat. But the mind, with the aid of language, does just this; and these detached and abstracted meanings are now available for translation and metaphor.

The body's manipulations and translations take place in the space and time which provide the framework for nature's existences. All of the body's manipulations are describable in terms of motion. The mind's translations and metaphors are evinced in a different medium. Through its acquaintance with this medium, which is that of its own life, the mind comes to exhibit an interest in types of order other than those manipulated in the space-time relation of nature's events. The discernment of relational structures, of types of necessity, of what I earlier called ideals of theoretic intelligibility, becomes possible; and the mind is led on to explore this new dimension of being. Guided by that which the mind discovers as it ranges over these meanings, the mind tries to see whether they are pertinent to all that it observes in the phenomenal manifold of nature and life. The mind is still engaged in a voyage of discovery, not sheer invention. It takes its cue from its own possessions, the immediacies of its own actual experience, and the data provided by its experiences. It finds these experiences to be conveyers and embodiments of meaning. These are the meanings which the mind manipulates.

Metaphor rests upon analogy. In transporting a meaning from one context to another the situation from which the meaning is detached bears some resemblance, some analogy, however tenuous, to the situation which becomes the new habitat of that meaning. The discernment of things which resemble one another predisposes the mind to try the experiment of carrying over some meaning from one thing to another.

The history of language is a long chapter in the story of what the mind does with its meanings. Just so, the development of man's practical arts and technologies is the story of what the body has done with the manipulanda supplied by nature. Of course these are not two wholly separate histories, yet they transpire in two different dimensions, the one that of space-time, the other that of the dimension in which the mind carries about and "metaphors" its meanings.

To the definition of man as *homo faber, homo sapiens, homo artifex, homo loquens, homo religiosus, homo ridens,* I would add one more, *homo transferens.* All of his powers, indicated by these other definitions, depend upon his ability to translate, upon the manipulations of his body and the metaphors of his mind. Man is the animal who translates. The history of the changes in the meanings of words, shown in the growth of language, provides instances of the mind transporting a meaning from one context to another, of the mind's activity of metaphoring. Let a few simple illustrations suffice.

A pivotal term in the history of the mind and of man's intellectual life is the word "idea." The word derives from the act of vision, from the seeing eye and what it beholds. The Latin *videre* retains this primitive meaning. What is seen at first is a visible shape or form clearly outlined against its background. An extant phrase of Democritus speaks of ἰδέαι οὐ ἀτομαί. The most important aspect of an atom is its shape, its "idea." The meaning of shape or form has been carried over, metaphored, from visible form to the shape of the invisible atom. But the process of translation and metaphor has but just begun. The Greeks first saw (again the metaphor of vision) that intellectual knowledge is the discernment of principles, laws, rhythms and patterns within the welter of nature's processes. These are now "ideas," envisioned by the mind's eye. Man's "art," "wisdom," and *Wissenschaft* are linguistic derivations of the bodily act of vision. The meaning embodied in the act of seeing is carried over to the intellectual apprehension of form and order. It would be difficult to exaggerate the range of meaning-transfers, of metaphors, derived from the act and apparatus of vision and the light which makes seeing possible, which have entered into the vocabulary of knowledge and intellectual activity. To conceive the mind as a mirror, *speculum,* held up to nature and thereby in speculation to discern the reflected images of things, to illumine what would otherwise be dark, to express one's insight with lucidity, to recognize perspectives—in these ways among many others has the metaphor of vision and light left its mark on the language in which we try to utter what it means to know. Only through metaphor has language, and the mind which is its author, been able to seize this thing called knowing. If there be a hidden wisdom in the body, enabling it to carry on with such marvelous precision and subtlety the manifold activities requisite for its own life, is there not an analogous wisdom embodied in language, even more subtle and more ethereal than any of the body's manipulations?

I have spoken of the body. The mind has done an extraordinary thing with the old English word which means "body." The earliest English or Saxon word for the human body, living or dead, is *lyke*. But see what this ancient bodily *lyke* has become! The things that are *likable,* and that we *like,* things that are *like* one another, thus yielding the basis for all analogy and all metaphor, and the injunction to be *like*-minded—by what subtle alchemy did the old bodily *lyke* become transmuted into things of the mind and the spirit? Some meaning and content of the body must have become loosened from its embodiment there, captured, and set free to find another embodiment elsewhere. We are still, of course, in the realm of metaphor, but that is our present theme, for the mind is that which metaphors and translates.

None of this activity of translating, of metaphoring meanings, could go on if things were not given us as having meanings. These meanings become then the mind's possessions, to explore and to manipulate. The mind has need to interpret all that is given to it in experience; all given data come to us asking that we not only accept them but also respond to them and interpret them. This is the most basic thing which makes possible both life and knowledge. It will be set forth in different languages depending on the metaphor chosen. Some metaphors carry further than others; they succeed better in capturing and translating the meaning which we are after. But the mind's interpretation of the given never consists wholly in tacking on to the given an extraneous and adventitious meaning, determined by the mind's own interest, caprice, or structure. Interpretation is a mode of discovery. The mind is the place where the meanings belonging to the given become revealed, where the given has a chance to tell its own story and not be compelled to listen to a story invented by the mind. There is some aspect of discovery in all invention and all creativeness, in all judgment and all reasoning.

The fact that data, sensa, and any other given come to us with meanings makes possible abstraction and classification. Thus when I say that this patch of color is green, I am recording the fact that the quality of greenness is of a kind which has appeared and which may appear in innumerable instances. It is not simply a *this,* here and now present and possessed in sheer immediacy. It is also a *such,* a kind and type, a universal, capable of indefinite repetition, exemplification, and embodiment. This is more than any artifice of language. This use of language reports and discovers something. Language, like the body, has its wisdom. Possibility is being discovered here, and new worlds and dimensions are opening before the mind when it discovers that every *this* and *that* is also a *such.* What is actually possessed, here and now, becomes a window through which the mind may look beyond. Linguistically, this is the domain of adjectives and of common nouns. This entity now had in experience is recognized as a member of a class. No logical gulf separates membership in a class, and existing as an instance of a law. The formulation of a law of nature but carries further the kind of thing we do when we recognize an object as being of such and such a kind, as belonging to a class. To identify this illness as a case of measles is no different in principle from identifying the tides as an instance of the law of gravitation. Classification and the classificatory sciences are more at home in a world which stays put, a world of fixities in space, rather than in one of events and changes in time. The sciences, concerned with happenings in time, with events, do for them what the classificatory sciences do for things in space. But both are employed, fundamentally, with the same kind of meaning. They are based upon the capacity of one particular item, whether object or event, to be the purveyor of a meaning which transcends its own particularity.

This is the type of meaning with which scientific knowledge is chiefly, if not exclusively, concerned. There is another order of meaning, still within man's cognitive experience, which demands notice. What this is may become evident by way of contrast with one feature of the generic concept, whether class or law. The common noun "dog" denotes the class of all dogs. There are many varieties of dogs and very many individual dogs, all belonging to a single class. A mongrel cur is just as truly a dog as a highly bred prizewinner in a dog show, so far as the defining characters of the class dog are concerned. With respect to these canine qualities, by virtue of which any dog belongs to the class dog, all members of the class are on a par. No one individual dog is any more of a dog, or any more adequate exemplification of the type dog, than is any other. Descriptive classification is democratic and leveling. The same holds good, *mutatis mutandis,* in dealing with instances of a law. If the tides and the fall of a stone are instances of the law of gravitation, and treated as such, there is no warrant for saying that one of them is a better exemplification, a more perfect conveyor of what the law means, than the other. All instances participate on equal terms in the type, class, or law of which they are particular instances. Here is a bond which links the scientific temper with that of democracy. The generic concept brooks no hierarchy among the items taken as belonging to the class under which they are subsumed.

There are, however, situations in which meanings are employed in a different way and in which they play another role. This may be illustrated in the case of science itself. Science, like dog, may be taken as a class concept. There are many varying instances of science, just as there are many different dogs. There is the science of the early Greek thinkers, the physics and biology of Aristotle, of the Renaissance, of Kepler, Galileo, and Newton, and of contemporary nuclear physics. There is meteorology and bacteriology and seismology, archeology, anthropology, and psychology. You cannot exclude primitive science or the grossly inadequate physics of Aristotle from the generic concept of science. If the sciences which are now judged to be primitive and inadequate are excluded from the class science, one is barred from inquiring into and speaking of the historical development of science. But science has a history. It had to shake itself loose from magic and animism. It has grown from feeble and floundering beginnings to its present magnificent structure, and the end is not yet. Imperfect sciences and inadequate stages in the development of science are all included in the generic class science, and they are all there on equal terms. But, unlike the class dog, where any dog is as much a dog as any other, there are some instances of science which, we suppose, have less right to claim the title than others. There are some sciences, some stages in the history of science, which incorporate or convey the meaning of science less adequately than others. The idea of science functions as an ideal meaning in which all the instances of science do not participate on equal terms. The descriptive class concept is poorly adapted to ascertaining and defining the essential nature of science. The meaning of science is normative and prescriptive. Instead of a generic idea, we have an ideal.

A similar situation is present in all of the other massive interests and activities which pertain to man's history and experience. Where various items are comprised within a class there is no objective basis for the judgment that one item is a better instance of the class than another. The only possibility is to fall back on what anyone happens to like. The case is different when we have particular items which vary with respect to their adequacy as embodiments and conveyors of meanings. There are regions of man's experience which are not to be understood in terms of description, classification, and generic explanation. Socrates was puzzled as to whether there was a form or idea of hair and of dirt. These are class concepts, and one kind of dirt participates as fully as another in the generic class. But he had no doubt whatever about justice. Here is an ideal meaning which various instances of justice may more or less imitate. They participate unequally in the essential nature of justice. They differ as to their adequacy as bearers and embodiments of the meaning of justice. Justice is not a class concept.

I see in all this a paradigm, an analogy, a kind of metaphor of what transpires throughout all the ranges of man's experience. Meanings are generated in human experience. They are conveyed by every possession of his mind. When released from the circumstances in which they are born, they assume the role of critic and judge. The mind uses these meanings to appraise the adequacy of the vehicles which embody and convey them. Why should the mind translate and convey a meaning from one situation to another, unless it felt dissatisfied with the capacity of some one of its particular possessions adequately to contain that meaning? Visible shape cannot convey all that its own meaning demands. The word "idea" which at first denoted visible form outgrows the limitation which circumscribed its primitive use. The contours seen by the bodily eye suggest a meaning which has to find elsewhere a vehicle more commensurate with its own implications. The history of the growth of language, of the meaning changes which words undergo, is a scroll left behind by the mind's effort to capture the full scope of meanings suggested by its experience. The physical body does not exemplify all of the meaning which it suggests, and the old *lyke* which meant body is sublimated into meanings which seem to have lost all connection with the palpable thing which first conveyed that meaning. Language itself arose because gross physical objects, such as were carried on the backs of Swift's projectors in Lagado, were so hopelessly inadequate to convey and to embody the meanings which clamored for expression and utterance. Literal conveying and translation of manipulanda in the medium of space was supplanted by metaphorical translation of meanings in the medium of mind.

The word "content" has just been used. Here is another metaphor which has been employed in language about the mind. The mind is a container, and there are contents of consciousness and of mind. This is something different from the mind as owner. The books which I own are not contained within me, as pennies are held within the purse which contains them. The possessions of the mind need not be its constituents. But the metaphor of container and content is significant when it comes to meanings. Meanings, as they are found and used in man's life and history, are contained in something, held within a shell which encapsulates them. Here is the root and the source of a significant contrast and tension pervading all of man's life and history. Meanings outgrow their containers. The restless search for more adequate embodiments of the mind's meanings provides the clue to an understanding of the history both of language and of all of the massive, typical expressions of human interests and activities. We name them "institutions." For what is an institution but a structure contrived to house and to contain a meaning? What is a word but the container and embodiment of a meaning? Institutions change because they are no longer able to sustain and to house some meaning which they would incorporate and contain. The meaning is the norm and standard of the structure which houses and expresses it. The metaphor of content and container, of inner and outer, has proved to be indispensable in understanding the historical career of human life. This metaphor is not yielded by anything supplied from within the observer's perspective. Correlations among coexistences and sequences, deployed within a single-dimensional phenomenal manifold, provide no habitat for structures which contain and embody meanings.

The mind uses its meanings to judge the adequacy of the structures, the institutions, the words, which are the containers of just these same meanings. In doing this the mind reenacts, in its own history, a drama analogous to that which was enacted within nature when mind itself appeared. To say that mind put in an appearance in the course of nature's history is itself a metaphor. Nature is a stage, and mind appears as a new actor. Where the actor came from, what he may have been doing before his stage appearance, or whether he is, indeed, not any new actor but an old one putting on a different mask, raise questions which at the moment may be left unanswered. Recognizable mind, the kind we take ourselves to be familiar with, presumably put in its appearance when animal bodies had reached a certain level of development and complexity. The birth of conscious experience is shrouded in darkness. Life at least there certainly was, before the coming of mind.

But there are myriad forms of life, of flower and tree, of vertebrate, crustacean, and mollusk, of coelenterate and protozoan, down to bacteria and the filterable viruses. Is all this life an affair wholly of physics and chemistry; or does it harbor something resembling recognizable mind, some sort of near-mind, making of it nature's bridge from sheer physico-chemical things and processes to those animal bodies in conjunction with which recognizable mind may indubitably be found? The story of life before recognizable life appears may plausibly be read in either way. Sherrington is confident that the boundary between the lifeless and the living is wholly factitious and conventional. Both the living and the lifeless are energy systems presenting no essential differences that cannot be accounted for in terms of the rearrangments of their ultimate constituents. Nature is constantly reshuffling the elements at her disposal. She is the great manipulator.

She does blindly, without forethought, what man does purposively in translating the manipulanda which surround him. In living forms the elements enter into new and different relations with one another, but such appearance of new types of order and organization characterize nature throughout. Given energy and motion, time and space, the

stage is set for an infinity of organizational relations, all deployed in the spatio-temporal medium. In none of the
resulting structures, including living bodies, is there any
observable entity in addition to the chemical elements plus
the ever-changing relations sustained between them. Life
surveyed in these terms (which are those of the life sciences)
reveals no prescience, no intent, no conations, no needs,
none of the meanings which require the medium of conscious experience for their enactment and existence. To
say that this plant "needs" water is but a way of saying that
a lack of water will be followed by chemical changes and
rearrangements which we designate as death. When I say
that the batteries of my car need to be recharged, I am im-
puting to the batteries no demand or conatus originating
in themselves. *I* have needs and wants because I have experience. The batteries have structure and organization;
they are moving systems and streams of physical energy in
space-time, and there are no scientific grounds for applying
to them any other categories than those of physics and
chemistry. For the understanding of biological phenomena,
no entities or elements not found in inanimate nature are
observable. There are new and different relational systems
into which these enter in the case of living things, and this
is all. But if life is a forerunner of mind, it ought to contain
something additional to its chemistry. A kind of no man's
land is here, something not yet mind, recognizable mind,
and yet more than physical structure and energy. The story
of biology, as I read it, is the elimination of all such go-
betweens. Vegetative souls and animal spirits have gone.
There remains but one great divide. On the one side, space-
time, matter and energy, physics and chemistry; on the
other side, mind and consciousness; and, even with the help
of metaphors supplied by our common sense and our sci-

ences, the language of one side is not readily translatable into the language of the other side.

As we try to imagine what this earliest mind was like, we shall think of it as hardly more than an echo, a resonance, and an expression of the life of the body. It is as if the activities of the body found utterance in sense, feeling, and impulse. The interests and energies of life had become too intense and exuberant to exhibit themselves solely in chemical reactions and bodily behavior. They overflow, break through the barriers of the body and the space-time, which is its habitat, and they burst forth, like the song of the nightingale. The mind which has now appeared is the entelechy of the body. The body's selectivity, its delicacy of response, finds an echo in a flash of sentiency which the animal momentarily experiences. To give precision to the theme that mind is the expression of the life of the body has been the concern of many a philosopher, done by no one in our time with such play of language and imagination as by Santayana. Metaphor after metaphor pours forth in his writings to convey something of what it means for the mind to be the body's entelechy. "The soul is the voice of the body's interests," conscious perception being "a private echo and response to ambient motions." With mind, "animal life which is a habit in nature bursts as with a peal of bells into a new realm of being, the realm of spirit." "Consciousness, in its genesis and natural status, is one of the indirect but inevitable outpourings proper to an existence which is in flux and gathers itself into living bodies. In consciousness, the psyche becomes festive, lyrical, rhetorical, she caps her life by considering it, and talking to herself about the absent parts of it." [1]

[1] George Santayana, *The Realm of Matter* (New York, 1930), p. 157 and *passim*.

The irrefragable continuity between mind and life con-
noted by the term "entelechy" and by these metaphors has,
at the very least, a unique quality exhibited nowhere else
in the flux of nature's processes. A terminal moraine is the
resultant of geological processes. We would not say, except
by a kind of metonymy, that it expresses the energies which
lie behind its formation and its structure. Nor are the rum-
blings of an earthquake a voice in which the strains beneath the earth's surface find expression and utterance. And
if life is, biologically, wholly an affair of chemistry, then
we ought to stick to the language of causality, of antecedents and consequences, and not read into life any residue
of meanings whose existence depends on conscious experience.

The category of *expression* is different from the category
of *causation*. If a sensation or feeling is said to be just as
much a natural event as is an earthquake, differing from it
solely in the nature of its antecedents and consequences
and in the space-time interactions with other events, then
there is something missed out. A visual sensation, as experienced, is the cumulative expression of a vast sweep of
energy transactions involving the object, the intervening
light waves or photons, chemical changes in the retina, a
transmission of electric charges across nerve fibers, and the
disturbance and redistribution of brain potentials. The
simplicity of the sensory quality as felt masks an infinite
complexity and conspiracy of surrounding objects, body,
sense organ, and brain. If the sensation were merely the last
event in a causal chain, stretching from distant object to
brain disturbance, it would be just that brain disturbance
and nothing more. Events which are causal antecedents
have vanished when their effects become manifest. The
sensation telescopes into a felt, simple quality; there is a

wealth of processes and energies, all of which find expression in the sensation. The sensation is an immediately experienced possession of the mind. It is at the same time the utterance and expression of interlocking strands of space-time events. This is its meaning, and mind appears as the medium in which the energies of nature are translated and transmuted into meanings.

But this is only the beginning, a halting first chapter in the story of the mind. I have spoken of visual sensations. There is one feature of visual experience which is noteworthy. Visual experience encompasses ranges of existence transcending those which pertain to the life and interests of the body. Through touch the animal is apprised of what is directly fateful for the body, physical things in immediate contact with its body. It becomes aware of what directly impinges upon its skin. The eye is a distance receptor. It gives warning of approaching dangers before they arrive. But in accomplishing this end vision discloses to the mind an endless array of distant objects, many or most of which have no bearing whatever upon the fate of the body. The development of vision is nature's earliest experiment in providing the mind with material which is not directly harnessed to the exigencies of the body. To number the stars and to order them in constellations evinces an interest transcending the body's fortunes. This artifice of nature, long antedating the advent of man, supplies a hint of what lies in store for the mind's future development. The biological utility of vision is obvious. I do not know the extent to which any animal other than man takes the hint, enjoys and explores the meanings of visual perception, of what is so distant as to have no practical bearing upon how his body is to behave. The animal mind is, presumably, the spokesman and guardian, the entelechy of the body. It is circumscribed by needs and interests focused in the life of the body. It has not achieved the capacity to detach itself from the circumstances of its origin, to develop its own interests and meanings, to transfer and translate these meanings from one embodiment to another.

As mind develops in this direction, it becomes less and less a complete account of its nature to describe it as the entelechy of the body. I come back to the analogy between the development of the mind within nature, and the play of meanings within the life of the mind itself. My theme is metaphor, translation, the setting free of a meaning from its original house and carrying it over to another and more adequate habitat. This is what happens in the growth of language. Meanings which are not class terms function as ideals by means of which the validity of its various embodiments is judged. It is the mind which carries on this activity of translating, just as the body is employed in the business of moving around manipulanda in space. Now the mind which can do this must itself have acquired a degree of freedom beyond that which any entelechy of the body could possess. Here is a kind of progressive disembodiment of the mind. This again is metaphor, and it has to reckon with the fact that, for us, the only recognizable mind is embodied mind. To speak of disembodiment is not to sanction ghosts and spooks. It is to remind us that the life of the mind which may have begun as the resonant echo of bodily activity outgrows the occasion which originally called it forth, and expands the orbit of its interests and concerns beyond anything which the body could achieve. It is like a content which needs some different and better container. The possibility of such detachment earmarks just that activity and attitude of being a spectator to which reference has been made.

The inadequacy of the body as the vehicle of the mind's purposes and interests is witnessed by all human technology. Tools and implements are extensions of the limbs of the body, enabling, as we say, the hand to chisel and paint and draw. But the unaided hand needs to be supplemented. By itself it is crude and weak. If man is a tool-making animal, he is so because he has discovered how feeble a vehicle and instrument is his body when measured against all of his conscious purposes and ends. And a machine which goes by itself, an automatic reaper or lathe, has almost entirely freed itself, once it is constructed, from the necessity of being guided by the human hand at all. A machine is the culmination of physical manipulanda. It is a disembodied mechanism, detached, that is, from the living body. A machine is an invention which has ceased to be geared to the routine of the body's rhythms. Contrived by the ingenuity of man, of many men, it is projected into space, there to go its own way and to pursue the logic of its own structure, threatening, Frankenstein-like, to sweep man's life within the orbit of its own energies.

This detachment of manipulanda which have become complex and mighty, this loosening of machines from the body which fashioned them, has its analogy with what happens to the mind's meanings when they, too, become compact and organized. They, too, are set free from the circumstances of their origin. A scientific observation, a discovery, or the making of a hypothesis is an episode in the biography of the scientist. It is an individual, historical achievement, dated and enmeshed in a particular local set of contingent circumstances. The historical traditions in which he lives, the social and economic needs of his time, the proclivities and prejudices which have conditioned the bent of his interests, the fortunate collocation of genes which make up his biological endowment, the quality of cells and associative fibers in his brain—all such factors and many others lie behind every discovery, hypothesis, and theory. His intellectual achievement is the fruition, a kind of entelechy, the cumulative expression of many interwoven strands and stretches of events in nature and history.

But science is an achievement of the mind. And mind is the medium in which meanings can get detached from the circumstances of their birth. Men have wanted their meanings, their ideas, to be shaken loose from the contingent and arbitrary, from the pressures which play upon them from behind, so that they may disclose the world as it is, and the ranges of being which lie within themselves. It is this which men call "reason." The mind becomes the judge of its own past and of the world which has given it birth. It becomes rebellious and wayward, often not knowing what to do with its freedom, in restless search for that which might be the adequate container and embodiment of its meanings. The mind which can embark upon the pursuit of science and of knowledge, of justice and happiness, is no longer quite the entelechy of the body. It is a mind which acknowledges claims laid upon it coming from a different direction from that in which lie all the vicissitudes of its body and of its past. Here is a tension of which all animals other than man would seem to be innocent. Man's life is fundamentally precarious not only because nature holds out so many goods which she soon snatches away, but because he lives at the crossroads of two dimensions. What I earlier called man's metaphysical sense is his recognition of just this.

Are spirit and nature, mind and body two, or are they one? In asking this question, it were wise to remember that one and two belong to language which pertains to things to be counted. Are we to set body and mind before us and, counting them, see whether we get one thing or two? Our minds are embodied and our bodies are ensouled. Yet the mind does that which the body cannot do. The body manipulates and transfers things. The mind discovers meanings, makes them its own, and then it metaphors them, uprooting them from their containers, ceaselessly seeking more adequate ones, and it thereby evinces its own freedom.

I think it needful never to forget the disparity between what the body does with its manipulanda and what the mind does with its meanings. Yet both of these are translatings, transferrings, and metaphorings, and the mind's employment of its meanings is a metaphor of the body's mastery of its manipulanda. How could this be unless both our experience and nature were embraced within a single world, a world not coinciding with either, and vastly richer in its content than anything displayed in our fragmentary minds and in the nature encompassed within our limited experience? It is man's metaphysical sense which impels him to ask this question and to draw upon all the resources of metaphor, symbol, and imagery to proffer an answer consonant with the entire range of meanings which his experience reveals. These chapters but provide the setting for this question and, like all metaphysical reflection, they leave us at the threshold of fresh and further inquiries.

Index

Abstraction and classification, 139 ff.

Academy of Projectors in Lagado, Swift's, 133

Accessibility, of being, 67 ff.; has become possession, 91, 92

Action, knowledge is not, 28

—— and life, 22 f.

Active tendencies, 113, 115

Activity, experience of, 88

Actual experience, 105

Aesthetic experience, 108 f.

Analogy, metaphor rests upon, 136; linguistic basis, 138

Animals, extent of awareness, 13; mind and experience ascribed to some, 100; extent of consciousness in behavior of, 116 f., 123

Animism, early, 70, 80; and nature, 122

—— perspective of, 81 ff., 90, 123; influence of observer's perspective (q.v.), 85, 86 ff.; experience in, 97; meaning a category derived from, 109, 110, 122; concept of active tendency, 113

Anticipatory meanings, 111 ff., 121

Aristotle, 5; metaphysics, 35, 37, 42, 43, 44, 60, 70, 71, 72, 83; physics, 141

Augustine, St., 35

Awareness, 106

Bacon, Francis, 9; quoted, 21

Becker, Carl, quoted, 14, 17

Beginnings and endings, 114

Behavior, 76

Being, categories of becoming and, 38; concept of: why neutral, 66; accessibility of, 67; prepositional quality imported into, 69; see also Existence; Life

Berkeley, George, 9

Body, animal: visual experience, 24, 137, 148 f.; relation between mind and: sign- and symbol-making mechanisms, 129; manipulations and translations, 130, 132, 135, 153; derivation and transmutation of word, 138, 143; mind as entelechy of, 147 ff.; inadequacy as vehicle of mind's purposes and interests, 150 f.; detachment of manipulanda, 151

Book, metaphysical exercise of reading and understanding, 63

Bradley, Francis H., 51

Browne, Sir Thomas, 40

Burnet, John, 81

Cartesian dualism, 98

Cassirer, Ernst, 81

Causation, Hume's account of, 115; difference between expression and, 148

Christian vocation, 35; theology, 37

Classification and abstraction, 139 ff.

Climate of opinion, as determinant of thinking, 14; deliquescence of metaphysical sense within, 43

Cognition, see Knowing

Common-divisor type of metaphysics, 72 ff.

Common sense, 46, 49

Concretions in existence and in discourse, 126

Consciousness, wonder of the birth of, 18; quality of experiencing designated by: distrust of, 77; why made indispensable and fundamental: mind and experience, 77 ff.; indefinability, 78; difficulty of disentangling ingredients of fact and theory, 79; perspective of animism (*q.v.*), 81 ff.; foundation and starting point for all knowledge, 82; and development of modern individualism, 84 ff.; observer's, over against animistic, perspective, 85, 86 ff.; revision of the nature and meaning of, 86; when made pivotal and ultimate, 90; accessibility, become possession, means conscious awareness, 91 ff.; evanescence and unsubstantiality, 92 ff.; yet is all that counts in life, 94; centrality of the problem of, and its results, 97 f.; relational theories of, 101; role played by, and relation between meaning and, 110 ff., 121; conscious events grouped and organized, 116; interpretation of nature in terms of conscious experience, 118; role of generating or using symbols, 128; *see also* Mind

Consummatory meanings, 111 ff., 121

Container and content, metaphor of, 143

Continuity and inclusiveness, role of search for, 47

Contrasts, *see* Dualities

Counting, activity of, 26

Data and the given (*q.v.*) in man's experience, 55 ff.

Democritus, 137

Descartes, René, 25, 83, 85, 88, 90, 98

Dewey, John, 86; quoted, 82

Differential equation, 115

Dingle, Herbert, quoted, 76

Discontent with the given, 56 f., 61

Discourse, relationship of metaphysics and, 67; rift between things and: propensity to speak in metaphor and parable, 126 f.; *see also* Language

Discovery, interpretation a mode of, 139

Dixon, W. M., quoted, 38

Dualities, contrasts, and tensions: ancient and traditional, in two-world theories, 36 ff.; experience and nature, 38 f.; the staple problems of philosophy, 40

Eddington's two tables, 60

Empiricism, modern, 9; philosophy of Hume, 9 f.; coalesces with naturalism, 30; doctrine of necessary relations, 61-64; appeal to experience, 66; loaded with phenomenalism, 87

Empiricists, the earlier classical, 9

Endings and beginnings, 114

Equation, functional, 114; differential, 115

Europe, influence of Greek philosophy (*q.v.*), 5; formative forces, 7; how metaphysical tradition has been carried along, 47; animism in history of thought, 80

Events, sequence of, 113 ff.; conscious, 115

Evidence, specific and objective, 13; philosophical beliefs due to factors other than, 13

Existence, analysis of meaning of: different modalities and dimensions found, 42 ff., 50, 51; contrasts in realm of, denoted by terms "nature," 49, 51 ff.; and "experience," 49; not limited by concept of being, 66; nature of, in ancient and in modern metaphysics, 67 ff.; greatest common divisor, 72 ff.; *see also* Being; Life

Experience, Greek view of depend-

ence upon knowledge and insight, 6; with life, now given primacy, 7, 66; meaning and content of term, 8, 66; relation of knowledge to, in ancient and modern view, 9; autonomy and ultimacy of, the premise of empiricism, 9, 66; and nature coalesce, 30; issues of metaphysics pivoted around the category of, 38, 96; stabilization of: a chief meaning of common sense, 46; concept and area of, 49 ff.; datum and gifts, 55 ff.; neutral meaning: the concept of being as such, 66 ff.; accessibility of being, 67; non-neutral meaning: contrast between entities which have, and do not have, experience, 70, 74 ff., 96; extraordinary usages of term, 76; possessor of, 77, 90, 94; concept of consciousness (*q.v.*), 77 ff.; perspectives of animism, 81 ff.; of observer, 86 ff. (*see entries under* Animism; Observer); phenomenalist interpretation, 87, 89; the immediately given, 103 ff.; ideal limits, 107; aesthetic, 108; meaning as a category of, 109; contrast between nature and, 110; sentient, 118; birth of conscious experience, 145; visual, 148, 149
Experiencing, activity of, 87
Experiment, 27
Explanation, necessity for, in the activity of scientific knowing, 60
Expression and causation, difference between, 148

Fact, *see* Matters of fact
Fallacy, of misplaced inclusiveness, 48 f., 50; of misplaced finality, 48 f., 53, 72; of reductionism, 71 f.
Finality, fallacy of misplaced, 48 f., 53, 72

Given, the: and datum, 55 ff.; discontent with, 57 f., 61; reason as

source, 57, 61; mind's interpretation of, 138 f.
Good, the: as the possessions of experience, 90
Greatest-common-divisor type of metaphysics, 72 ff.
Greek philosophy and philosophers, 4, 31, 69, 137; spectator view of knowledge, 5 ff.; rationalism, 6, 7; metaphysics, 9, 35-45 *passim*, 60, 67, 68, 70-83 *passim*; Humean conviction, antithesis of the Socratic, 10; science, 141; *see also names, e.g*, Socrates

Hegel, G. W. F., 48, 68, 85
Hobbes, Thomas, 128
Homo transferens, 136
Hume, David, 32; philosophy of, 9 f., 53, 61, 62, 64, 88; quoted, 73; treatment of impressions, ideas, 106; account of causality, 115

Idea, Locke's doctrine, 87, 90; Hume's, 106; a pivotal term: derivation, 137; early limitation outgrown, 143
Identification, activity of, 127
Immediacy, 102 ff.
Impressions, Hume's concept, 106
Inclusiveness, role of search for continuity and, 47; fallacy of misplaced, 48 f., 50
Indeterminacy, principle of, 24
Individual, enhanced sense of significance, 83 f., 89; status of medieval and modern concepts of, 84; reversal in respective roles of nature and: sense of power expressed in language of consciousness, 85; modern effort to safeguard: conscious experience the indispensable premise, 86, 98; meanings lent to life by nature, 121
Insight, life illumined with knowledge and, 4; dependence of life and experience upon, 6
Institutions, 144

Intention and meaning, 102
Interaction between knower and
known, absence of, 26

James, William, 86, 109, 128, 135;
meanings discovered in the stream
of thought, 111 ff., 118

Kant, Immanuel, 68
Knowing, the meaning, nature, and
intent of, 5; how activity of, now
viewed, 8; identification of vision
and cognition, 24; as one specific
function, 26; two extremes in
theory of, 55; pursued for purposes of prediction and control,
58; see also Mind
Knowledge, life illumined with insight and, 4; relationship between
life and, 4-33; spectator view, 5 ff.,
21 ff., 53; reversal of view, 7 f., 9;
relation to experience, in ancient
and modern view, 6, 9; now seen
ancillary to, and a phase and episode of, life and living, 7; conflicting interpretations of, 20; attainment and intent of, 21 ff.; as science, based upon observation,
53 ff.; data, or the given, in man's
experience, 55 ff.; scientific, defined, 60; intellectual, defined,
137; seized through metaphor, 138

Language, steeped in metaphor: literal for science, 125; disparity between discourse and things, 126,
127, 133; instrument for translating meanings, 134, 135; knowing
seized through metaphor, 138; abstraction and classification, 139 f.;
origin, 143
Lewis, C. I., 31
Liberalism, modern, 84
Life, relationship with philosophy,
3; with knowledge, 4-33; with experience, is now given primacy,
7 ff.; reversal of relative position
of knowledge and, 8, 9; root of

dualities and tensions between
them, 21; practice and action,
22 f.; as presented within perspective of observer, 29 ff.; myriad
forms: whether it harbors some
sort of mind, 145; as forerunner
of mind, 146 f.; see also Being; Existence; Mind
Locke, John, 9, 83, 85, 87, 89, 90
Lodge, Sir Oliver, 25

Machines, 151
Malebranche, Nicolas, 25
Man, see Individual
Manipulation, body's activities of,
130, 135, 143, 151, 153; out of
place when applied to meanings,
132; in physical nature, 134
Mathematics, 11; counting procedures, 27; symbols, 127
Matters of fact, whether necessary
relations between, 62 ff.
Mead, G. H., quoted, 116
Meaning, interplay of possession
and, 101 ff.; types, and their employment, 102, 140 ff.; derivation
of the category of, 109, 110; relation between consciousness and,
110 ff., 121; analysis of, in James's
"Stream of Thought," 111; nature
given meanings and meaningful
relations, 119 ff.; what mind does
with, 130, 132 ff. (see entries under
Mind); language the instrument
for translating, 134, 135; significance of the metaphor of container and content, 144
Mechanisms, sign- and symbol-making, 129
Mechanistic theories of nature, 79
Memory, 106; and anticipation, 112
Mental phenomena, conception of
mind in terms of, 101
Metaphor, language steeped in, 125;
resemblances the seeds of, 126; of
ownership, 127; derivation and
meaning, 131; a transferring
agency for mind, 131; its mean-

ings metaphored, 132 ff., 150; basis for analogy and, 138; Santayana's use of, 147; mind's employment of its meanings a metaphor of body's use of its manipulanda, 153

Metaphysics, 34-65; of the Greeks, 9, 35-45 *passim,* 60, 67, 68, 70-83 *passim;* nature of, 11; diversities and conflicts within: effect of factors that contribute to formation of, 15; lack of a settled middle territory, 19; origin and meaning of term, 35; contrast between life and its habitat, 36; source of problems in dualities, contrasts, and tensions, 36 ff.; why issues now pivoted around the category of experience, 38; historic kinship with religions, 41; question as to what distinguishes contrasts which do, and do not, evoke the metaphysical sense, 41 ff.; naturalistic: mistaken suppositions about man's metaphysical sense, 44; ingredients and drives within, 47 ff.; penetration of sense of, into activity of scientific knowing, 60; responsibility for discontent with the given, 61; necessary relations, 61 ff.; recognition of contrasts, dualities, and tensions, kept alive, 64; shift in pivotal center of, indicative of modern culture and mentality, 66; substitution of experience for being, 67; greatest-common-divisor type, 72 ff.; *see also* Philosophy

Meyerson, Emile, 127

Middle Ages, metaphysics, 37; status of the individual, 84

Mind, bondage to determinants, 14, 21; what mind is, 16; relation between the domain of nature and, 16 ff.; marvel of the birth of consciousness, 18; philosophy's effort to annul duality between nature and, 31 ff.; possessions, experi-

ences, role, 66-95; possessor of experience, 77; concept of consciousness, 78 ff.; subjectivism resulting from making accessible objects into possessions of, 89; immediate possessions, 91 ff.; integration within nature, 98 ff.; two divergent paths in modern philosophy, 99, 100; as region of relations and relational structures, 101; meanings possessed by, 102; meaning as a cateory of, 109; as spectator, 123, 150; its discourse and its excursive power, 125-53; as owner, 127, 132; role of generating or using symbols, 128; relation between body and, 129; what it does with its meanings, 130, 132 ff.; realm or dimension in which meanings are carried on and "metaphored," 132, 135 ff., 150 ff.; interpretation of the given, 138 f.; as container, 143; appearance of, in course of nature's history, 144 ff.; as entelechy of the body, 147 ff.; relation of visual experience to, 149; set free from circumstances of its origin, 150 ff.; *see also* Consciousness; Knowing

Naturalism, and anti-naturalism, 16 ff.; coalesces with empiricism, 30

Nature, relation of mind to, 16 ff., 99; coalesces with experience, 30; philosophy's effort to annul duality between mind and, 31 ff.; as the totality of existence and as that which embraces all that pertains to mind and spirit, 44; and experience, two contrasted areas of existence, 49; physical, or natural science, 51; concept and area of, 51 ff.; contrast between natural and supernatural, 51; why realm designated as, is best suited to cover entire range of existence, 52; double meaning: nature of ex-